COBOL WITH STYLE

PROGRAMMING PROVERBS

Hayden Computer Programming Series

COMPREHENSIVE STANDARD FORTRAN PROGRAMMING
James N. Haag

COMPREHENSIVE FORTRAN PROGRAMMING
James N. Haag

BASICS OF DIGITAL COMPUTER PROGRAMMING (Rev. 2nd Ed.)
John S. Murphy

BASIC BASIC: An Introduction to Computer Programming in BASIC Language
James S. Coan

ADVANCED BASIC: Applications and Problems
James S. Coan

DISCOVERING BASIC: A Problem Solving Approach
Robert E. Smith

BEGINNING FORTRAN: Simplified, 12-Statement Programming
John Maniotes, Harry B. Higley, and James N. Haag

ASSEMBLY LANGUAGE BASICS: An Annotated Program Book
Irving A. Dodes

PROGRAMMING PROVERBS
Henry F. Ledgard

PROGRAMMING PROVERBS FOR FORTRAN PROGRAMMERS
Henry F. Ledgard

COBOL WITH STYLE: Programming Proverbs
Louis J. Chmura and Henry F. Ledgard

SNOBOL: An Introduction to Programming
Peter R. Newsted

FORTRAN FUNDAMENTALS: A Short Course
Jack Steingraber

COBOL WITH STYLE

PROGRAMMING PROVERBS

LOUIS J. CHMURA
The Mitre Corporation

HENRY F. LEDGARD
University of Massachusetts

HAYDEN BOOK COMPANY, INC.
Rochelle Park, New Jersey

Library of Congress Cataloging in Publication Data

Chmura, Louis J
    COBOL with style.

    (Hayden computer programming series)
    Bibliography: p.
    Includes index.
    1. COBOL (Computer program language) I. Ledgard,
Henry F., date   joint author. II. Title.
QA76.73.C25C5   001.6'424   76-22759
ISBN 0-8104-5781-4

Printed in the United States of America

1	2	3	4	5	6	7	8	9	PRINTING
76	77	78	79	80	81	82	83	84	YEAR

FOREWORD

By necessity, computer science, computer education, and computer practice are all embryonic human activities, for they have existed for only a single generation. From the beginning, programming has been a frustrating black art, with individual abilities ranging from the excellent to the ridiculous and often exhibiting very little in the way of systematic mental procedure. In a sense, the teaching of programming through mistakes and debugging can hardly be regarded as legitimate university level course work. At the university level we teach such topics as the notion of an algorithm, concepts in programming languages, compiler design, operating systems, information storage and retrieval, artificial intelligence and numerical computation; but in order to implement ideas in any of these functional activities, we need to write programs in a specific language.

Students and professionals alike tend to be overly optimistic about their ability to write programs or to make programs work according to pre-established design goals. However, we are beginning to see a breakthrough in programming as a mental process. This breakthrough is based more on considerations of style than on detail. It involves taking style seriously, not only in how programs look when they are completed, but in the very mental processes that create them. In programming, it is not enough to be inventive and ingenious. One also needs to be disciplined and controlled in order not to become entangled in one's own complexities.

In any new area of human activity, it is difficult to foresee latent human capabilities. We have many examples of such capabilities: touch typing, speed writing, and 70-year-old grandmothers who drive down our highways at 70 miles an hour. Back in 1900 it was possible to foresee cars going 70 miles an hour, but the drivers were imagined as daredevils rather than as grandmothers. The moral is that in any new human activity one generation hardly scratches the surface of its capabilities. So it will be in programming as well.

The next generation of programmers will be much more competent than the first one. They will have to be. Just as it was easier to get into college in the "good old days," it was also easier to get by as a programmer in the "good old days." For this new generation, a programmer will need to be capable of a level of precision and productivity never dreamed of before.

This new generation of programmers will need to acquire discipline and control, mainly by learning to write programs correctly from the start. The debugging process will take the new form of verifying that no errors are present, rather than the old form of finding and fixing errors over and over (otherwise known as "acquiring confidence by exhaustion"). Programming is a serious logical business that requires concentration and precision. In this discipline, concentration is highly related to confidence.

In simple illustration, consider a child who knows how to play a perfect game of tic-tac-toe but does not know that he knows. If you ask him to play for something important, like a candy bar, he will say to himself, "I hope I can win." And sometimes he will win, and sometimes not. The only reason he does not always win is that he drops his concentration. He does not realize this fact because he regards winning as a chance event. Consider how different the situation is when the child *knows* that he knows how to play a perfect game of tic-tac-toe. Now he does not say, "I hope I can win." He says instead, "I know I can win; it's up to me!" And he recognizes the necessity for concentration in order to insure that he wins.

In programming, as in tic-tac-toe, it is characteristic that concentration goes hand-in-hand with justified confidence in one's own ability. It is not enough simply to know how to write programs correctly. The programmer must *know that he knows* how to write programs correctly, and then supply the concentration to match.

This book of COBOL proverbs is well suited to getting members of the next generation off to the right start. The elements of style discussed here can help provide the mental discipline to master programming complexity. In essence, the book can help to provide the programmer with a large first step on the road to a new generation of programming.

HARLAN D. MILLS

Federal Systems Division, IBM
Gaithersburg, Maryland

PREFACE

This short text is a direct descendant of two earlier texts by one of us, *Programming Proverbs* (for ALGOL and PL/I programmers) and *Programming Proverbs for FORTRAN Programmers*. Those two texts were in turn motivated by a small book called *Elements of Style*, written by William Strunk, Jr. and revised by E. B. White. Originally conceived in 1918, Strunk's book stressed the need for rigor, conciseness, and clarity in the writing of English prose. In like manner, *COBOL with Style* is intended for COBOL programmers who want to write carefully constructed, readable programs.

Many programmers have told us of programming experiences in which a simple set of guidelines could have averted disaster. Although a burned hand may teach a good lesson, we believe that the introduction of well-advised guidelines is an easier and less painful way to learn good programming. To be sure, rules of style restrict the programmer. However, our hope is to enable the programmer to focus creativity on the deeper issues in programming rather than on problems that obscure the issues.

Several characteristics other than academic ones have been deliberately sought for in this book. First, there has been an attempt to be lighthearted. The intention is to encourage a zest for learning that we all need to do our more rewarding work. Second, there has been an attempt to be specific. Progress is made when we speak plainly and give examples for what we say.

The programming examples are given in COBOL, but the points of the examples should be clear even without a detailed knowledge of the COBOL language. In particular, the programs given here conform to the 1974 ANSI version of the COBOL language [Ref. Z1].* Those readers familiar only with a particular implementation of COBOL will notice some minor differences.

This book is designed as a guide to better COBOL programming, not as an introduction to the details of the COBOL language. It should be of value to all programmers who have some familiarity with COBOL. As such, it may be used as a supplementary text in courses where COBOL programming is a major concern, or as an informal guide to experienced COBOL programmers who have an interest in improving software quality. However, we strongly believe that the ideas presented should go hand-in-hand with learning the COBOL language itself.

*See the Bibliography at the conclusion of the text for all references.

The reader who dismisses the overall objective of this book with the comment, "I've got to learn all about COBOL first," may be surprised to find that the study of good programming practices in conjunction with the basics of the language may reap quick and longstanding rewards.

COBOL with Style is organized in five major parts. Chapter 1 is an opening statement. Chapter 2 is a collection of simple rules, called *proverbs*. The proverbs summarize in terse form the major ideas of this book. Each proverb is explained and applied. There are a few references to later chapters where various ideas are more fully explored.

Chapter 3 is an introduction to a strict top-down approach for programming problems in any programming language. The approach is oriented toward the easy writing of complete, correct, readable programs. It should be read carefully, because some of its details are critical and not necessarily intuitive. The approach hinges on developing the overall logical structure of the program first. Specific decisions, such as data representation or intermediate algorithms, are delayed as long as possible in order to achieve maximum flexibility.

Chapter 4 gives a set of strict program standards for writing programs. These rules have been strictly followed in this book, and we believe that their adoption is one of the most important factors in achieving quality programs. Chapter 5 elaborates on several important and sometimes controversial ideas discussed in the chapter on programming proverbs.

Our efforts have been aided by many individuals. Above all, William Cave and Michael Marcotty profoundly influenced our ideas. William Cave provided wisdom, experience, and provocative discussions during the entire effort. Michael Marcotty set an example of eloquent programming style and often contributed the right word at the right time. Edwina Carter, Gail Michael, and Linda Strzegowski provided services without which this book would be but a collection of handwritten pages without a title.

William Fastie, Joseph Davison, and Leslie Chaikin were the source of many ideas taken from the predecessors of this book. George Baird, John Burch, Angel Grindon, Dave Hastings, Joseph Kasprzyk, Ted Los, Andrew Singer, Michael Spier, Joe Sullivan, and Robert Taylor aided us in diverse ways. Members of the Computer and Information Science Department of the University of Massachusetts provided a solid intellectual environment for this work. Colleagues of the MITRE Corporation, Bedford, Massachusetts, provided expert opinion and a reader's fine eye. Finally, members of the U.S. Army Electronics Division at Forth Monmouth, New Jersey, provided a laboratory for many of our ideas. We are grateful to all.

COBOL with Style is surely our own personal statement about the art of programming. However, we are committed to the idea that the study of guidelines for good programming can be of great value to all programmers, and that there are principles that transcend the techniques of any individual practitioner.

LOUIS J. CHMURA, JR.
HENRY F. LEDGARD

CONTENTS

COBOL WITH STYLE

PROGRAMMING PROVERBS

CHAPTER ONE
THE WAY AHEAD

Things is 'round to help learn COBOL programmers, especially them who don't want to pick up no more bad habits, to program good, easy, the first time right, and so somebody else can figger out what they done and why.

For those readers who appreciate diamonds in the rough, the paragraph above represents all that follows.

An indication of the current state-of-the-art of computer programming is that the proud exclamation "It worked the first time!" is rarely heard. Writing programs that work correctly the first time is possible, but unusual. Since programmers undoubtedly try to write programs that work the first time, one wonders why they don't succeed more often. The reasons are simple. First, programming is difficult. Second, there are very few principles for developing and writing good programs. Since few principles exist, each programmer must develop individual ones, often haphazardly.

In reality, the state-of-the-art is considerably worse than the fact that most COBOL programs do not work right the first time. Too many programs work only most of the time. Indeed, a few never work at all. Most important, of those that do work correctly, many are laborious to maintain.

There has recently been an increasing concern within the computing community about the quality of software. As a result a new methodology is emerging, a harbinger of further changes to come. Notable are the works of Dijkstra, Mills, Wirth, Hoare, Weinberg, Wulf, Horning, Cave, Strachey, Kosaraju, Knuth, and Marcotty.

Many of the developing ideas are useful now. The time has come for programmers to write programs that work correctly the first time. Programs should do the whole job, even if the original problem has been poorly conceived. Programs should be easy to read, understand, and maintain.

For those accustomed to weeks of testing, poor program performance, or long hours deciphering someone else's code, the above statements might seem

1

unrealistic. Nevertheless, there are well-founded principles that can be utilized to achieve these goals. Some of the principles we shall present are obvious, even to novice programmers. Others even experienced COBOL programmers might debate. However, before any principle is rejected, it must be remembered that a COBOL program is not only a set of descriptions and instructions for a computer, but a *set of descriptions and instructions that must be understood by human beings, especially the one who reads it the most—you, the programmer.*

It is well known that the cost of program development and maintenance today is high and growing. In fact, we have heard it said that the cost of program maintenance on some poorly constructed systems is a hundred times greater than the cost of initial development and testing. To attack these costs, methodology and clarity must be early programming concerns.

In view of today's increasing development and maintenance costs and the decreasing costs of computer hardware, it is shortsighted to be overconcerned with various "micro-efficiency" [Ref. A1] techniques that save bytes and milliseconds. The considerations of an "efficient" computer program can no longer ignore over-all program costs.

The use of flowcharting as a program development and documentation technique also has been misunderstood and overestimated. A case against program flowcharts is given in Chapter 5. While judicious use of certain types of flowcharts can be a valuable part of the programmer's repertoire, there are numerous other programming techniques that have little need for flowcharts. The reader will observe a scarcity of program flowcharts in this book.

The development of effective algorithms and data structures is an activity that is closely tied with programming techniques. While programming techniques can offer strong guidelines for the development of a good solution, they will not necessarily help the programmer determine the best file organization scheme or best check digit method. The following pages concentrate on programming techniques.

CHAPTER TWO
PROGRAMMING PROVERBS

"Experience keeps a dear school, but fools will learn in no other."
Maxim prefixed to *Poor Richard's Almanack*, 1757

Over two centuries ago Ben Franklin published his now familiar *Poor Richard's Almanack*. In it he collected a number of maxims meant as a simple guide to everyday living. Similarly, this chapter is intended as a simple guide to everyday COBOL programming. As such it contains a collection of terse statements that serve as a set of practical rules for the COBOL programmer. These programming proverbs motivate the entire book.

Before going on, a prefatory proverb seems appropriate:

Do Not Break the Rules Before Learning Them

As with most maxims or proverbs the rules are not absolute, but neither are they arbitrary. Behind each one lies a generous nip of thought and experience. We hope the programmer will seriously consider them. At first glance some of them may seem either trivial or too time-consuming to follow. However, we believe that experience will prove the point. Just take a look at past errors and then reconsider the proverbs.

The programming proverbs, like all old saws, overlook much important detail in favor of easily remembered phrases. Indeed there are some cases where programs should not conform to standard rules; that is, there are exceptions to every proverb. Nevertheless, we think experience will show that these exceptions are rare, and that a programmer should not violate the rules without serious reasons.

A list of all the proverbs is given in Table 2.1. It is hard to weigh their relative importance, but they do at least fall into certain categories. The relative importance of one proverb over another depends quite markedly on the programming problem at hand.

Table 2.1   The Programming Proverbs

A Good Start is Half the Race

1. Don't Panic!
2. Define the Problem Completely.
3. Start the Documentation Early.
4. Think First. Code Later.
5. Proceed Top-Down.
6. Beware of Other Approaches.

Keeping Logical Structure

7. Code in Logical Units.
8. Use PERFORM and CALL.
9. Don't GO TO.
10. Prettyprint.

Coding the Program

11. Comment Effectively.
12. Use Mnemonic Words.
13. Get the Syntax Correct Now.
14. Plan for Change.
15. Don't Leave the Reader in the Dust.
16. Prepare to Prove the Pudding.

And of Course

17. Have Someone Else Read the Work.
18. Read the Manual Again.
19. Don't Be Afraid to Start Over!

We close this introduction by noting why we use the word *proverb*, rather than the more accurate word *maxim*. Proverbs and maxims both refer to pithy sayings derived from practical experience. Proverbs are usually well known, whereas maxims are usually not. Admittedly, our programming proverbs are not popular sayings. However, the title was chosen with an eye to the future, when hopefully some of these sayings might become true programming proverbs. And, of course, we think that "Programming Proverbs" just sounds better!

Proverb 1 DON'T PANIC

This is the first, but often overlooked, programming proverb. When given a new problem to solve, there are many forces that encourage the programmer to abandon thoughtful and effective programming techniques in favor of quicker, high-pressure, unproven ones. Typically, the programmer may be loaded down with other work. Management may be putting on the pressure by setting an unrealistic schedule or by promising a bonus for finishing early. Of course, there is always the natural human tendency to "get on with the job," or in other words, code. Unfortunately, the tendency to try to obtain speedy results is counter to good programming practice.

At the beginning of a programming project, the programmer's good sense must prevail. He or she must develop a thoughtful approach that ensures that the entire programming job is firmly in hand. Not doing so will surely result in a programming environment that is all too common today, where existing code is constantly being reworked as new code shows oversights, bugs hide all over the finished code, and maintenance takes much longer than expected.

If you find yourself upset or ploughing ahead with a new programming assignment,

1. Stop.
2. Calm down.
3. Return to methodical programming techniques.

We can't emphasize this enough! One of us, in fact, wanted to go further and retitle this proverb "TAKE THE AFTERNOON OFF," but you know what happens to ideas like that.

Proverb 2 DEFINE THE PROBLEM COMPLETELY

Good problem definitions are vital to the construction of good programs. An incomplete or ill-formed definition implies that the complete structure of the problem is not fully understood. Missing information, ignorance of special cases, and an abundance of extraneous information in a definition are good signs of poor programs, or at the best, of programs that will be a surprise for the ultimate user. Any program that processes large amounts of data is bound to encounter some simple unnoticed condition, resulting in the all too common program crash.

We have often heard the claim that it is quite permissible to start with an imperfect problem definition, for during later program development a good programmer will readily pick up any critical points missed in the initial definition. We strongly disagree with this view. Starting with solid, complete (albeit laborious) problem definition is often half the solution to the entire problem. Moreover, good definitions can serve as the basis for good program documentation.

There are many reasons why good problem definitions are rare. First, there is no well-accepted idea of what comprises a good definition. Different programmers and managers usually employ different definition techniques. For example, some project managers require only program narratives, decision tables, or system flowcharts. Another common practice is to have an experienced system analyst draw up several system flowcharts, some narrative descriptions, and some detailed descriptions of some inputs and outputs. Of course, the quality and completeness of these definitions will vary according to the style of the individual analyst.

Second, there is an almost irresistible temptation to skirt over the issue of definition in order to "get on with the job." This temptation is especially acute when the given problem is similar to previously solved problems or when there is strong external pressure to produce some quick, visible results (that is, programs). Furthermore, even if programmers could avoid the rush to get on with the job, management and the "customer" often make it difficult to invest the time and money for a good problem definition. The results of good definitions often appear to be wasted, since working code is usually delayed, especially when a programmer works hard to insure that no problem situations go unnoticed.

Third, good program definitions involve plain hard work. There is an intense amount of persistence and discipline required to get any definition straight.

Consider Example 2.1, an overly simplistic initial description of a problem. Most programmers, realizing the superficiality, would soon gather more facts about the problem and construct a much better problem definition, as shown in Example 2.2 and Fig. 2.1.

While the narrative and system flowchart problem definition provided by Example 2.2 and Fig. 2.1 are definite improvements, they suffer from several deficiencies. First, look at the input specification. By reading the narrative we can piece together a picture of the input NEW-MISSING-PERSONS file. But why not simply supply the picture directly as in Fig. 2.2, where all the specifications are given in a clear, compact form. The same type of picture can be drawn for the output NEW-MISSING-PERSONS file on disk storage.

Second, there is no detailed picture of the output report. The programmer who starts coding with only the definition of Example 2.2 will eventually have to plan and specify this output, having to interrupt coding to do so.

Third, consider the system flowchart in Fig. 2.1. Neither the system flowchart nor the narrative of Example 2.2 directly states whether there is a need for input validation and plausibility checks on the tape label and data record items. There is no mention whether there is a required day of the week

Example 2.1   A Typical Poor Initial Problem Description

Write a program to copy the NEW-MISSING-PERSONS file to disk storage and generate a report on the size of the file.

Example 2.2   A Second Pass at Problem Definition

The input file, NEW-MISSING-PERSONS, is a sequential file of new missing person records on magnetic tape. Each of these records has the following format:

Bytes	Contents
$1 \rightarrow 9$	Social Security Number
$10 \rightarrow 500$	Alphanumeric Data

The file is ordered on ascending value of social security number. The file is stored on magnetic tape with a blocking factor of 2. There is a tape label NMP-**, where ** represents an integer from 01 to 12.

The output file NEW-MISSING-PERSONS is a copy of the input file. The file is to be stored on IBM 3330 disk storage with a blocking factor of 2. Of course, this file is also ordered on increasing social security number field. The tape label should be copied over as a disk file label. The number of records on the input tape must be counted and the result reported out on line printer 01. We can presume that the input tape is compatible with our IBM system since it is prepared at an outside IBM installation. A system flowchart is given (see Fig. 2.1).

The general nature of our solution is the following:

> *read* a NEW-MISSING-PERSONS record from tape
> *write* that record to disk
> *add* one to the Record-Count
> *if* there are more input records
> > *then* go back and repeat this process
> > *else* terminate this program.

The program is scheduled for completion by week's end.

on which the tape is to be copied, or whether a clearance is required for program execution. Future expansion and problem generality are also ignored.

Fourth, the problem of Example 2.2 is partly defined by a specific algorithm stating the order of the calculations. This kind of definition should be

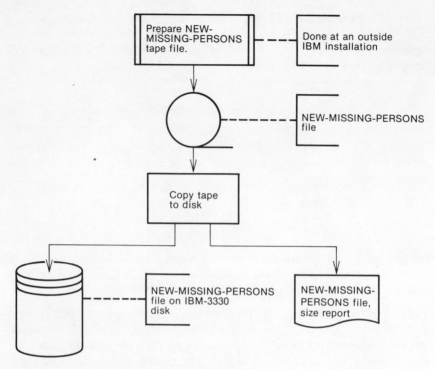

Fig. 2.1   System flowchart supplied with Example 2.2

avoided unless the implementation of a specific algorithm is actually part of the problem, because specification of an unnecessary algorithm clouds a problem specification by restricting the class of possible solutions.

In Chapter 3 we will discuss several ideas for producing good problem definitions in conjunction with a complete example. However, there are a few points about good definition that deserve to be mentioned here. First, in attempting to supply a complete problem definition, the programmer probably cannot err by devoting a great deal of time and thought. While perfect definitions are probably unattainable, with good technique and discipline you will end up "close" to one. Remember that all languages have rigid rules for the execution of programs, and programmers must be specific to the last detail. If something is left unspecified in the original definition, the programmer will eventually have to face the consequences. At best, the changes that must be made are frustrating and distracting.

Once you believe that a definition is complete, put it aside for a time. Pick it up later, and carefully reread and rethink it. Better still, have someone else read it (see Proverb 17). "Complete" problem definitions have been known to show flaws in the light of a new day.

As a final word, make sure that you have a complete *written* description of the problem before you do anything else.

NEW-MISSING-PERSONS FILE

Records are ordered by ascending value of SOCIAL SECURITY
NUMBER, and the label consists simply of an ID with value from
NMP-01 to NMP-12.

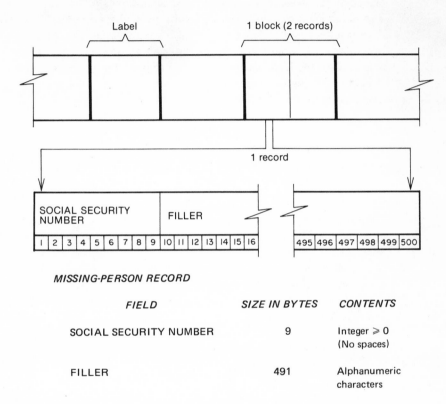

MISSING-PERSON RECORD

FIELD	SIZE IN BYTES	CONTENTS
SOCIAL SECURITY NUMBER	9	Integer $\geqslant 0$ (No spaces)
FILLER	491	Alphanumeric characters

Fig. 2.2 A picture specification of the input NEW-MISSING-PERSONS file

Proverb 3 START THE DOCUMENTATION EARLY

What can we say in one short proverb about a subject that has been
discussed, written about, and cursed at for years? Many have tried to define,
motivate, and analyze good data processing documentation, the central purpose
of which is to provide effective communication of factual information among
people.

Good documentation procedures have several characteristics:

1. *Readability is the chief goal.* Documentation is meant to be read by
   human beings. With good documentation, the reader does not have to

stare at a shelf of material with no idea where to begin. The reader obtains exactly the information required, no more and no less.

2. *Documentation is based on good standards.* The what, when and how of good documentation are recorded somewhere (i.e., standardized), and help is available to understand the standards.

3. *The required documentation is planned from the beginning.* Some documents are written long before others and serve as guides for the later ones. An efficient secretarial staff and automated aids exist to help manage the load. There is an active central library service, which manages both ongoing and completed project documentation.

4. *Documentation is part of the daily programming process.* Finger-paralyzing treatises on long forgotten topics are not needed. The documentation system drives the programming process!

5. *The procedures are carefully followed.* There is no pressure to skimp on documentation. Someone asks for needed documentation; someone reads it; and there is reward for producing high quality documentation.

Being honest men, we must admit to finding few documentation systems as good as all this. It is possible to be involved in a programming project with a less than perfect documentation system. In this event, you should develop your own ideas and procedures early.

We should all be able to recognize good data processing documentation. The only thing left to do is to begin to provide it. While you may not achieve a good documentation system right away, a step in that direction is far better than the confusion that exists in some places now.

Proverb 4   THINK FIRST, CODE LATER

This proverb is intimately connected with the previous proverbs. After you have settled on the problem definition and documentation procedures, the essential task is to start thinking about the solution as soon as possible, and to start the actual coding process only after you have devised a clear plan of attack.

Consider carefully the wording of this proverb: *Think first* means *think—do not code!* Start thinking while the problem is fresh in your mind and the deadline is as far away as it will ever be. Consider at least two different ways to solve the problem. Examine the approaches in sufficient detail to discover possible trouble spots or areas in which the solution is not transparent. A top-notch program requires a top-notch algorithm.

Code later means *delay coding*. Give yourself some time to weed out difficult parts and polish the algorithm before trying to formalize it in COBOL code. It is much easier to discard poor thoughts than poor programs.

A common violation of this proverb lies in the approach to programming that we shall call the "linear" approach. In the linear approach, a programmer receives a problem and immediately starts preparing the code to solve it. Avoid this temptation, for it is full of hidden costs and dangers. You will certainly feel foolish continuously revising an ill-conceived program, or in the extreme case, writing a program that already exists on your system.

In conclusion, remember Murphy's second law of programming: It always takes longer to write a program than you think. A corollary might be: The sooner you start coding the program (instead of thinking about it), the longer it will take to finish the job.

Proverb 5   PROCEED TOP-DOWN

A major objective of this book is to advocate the "top-down" approach to programming problems. The top-down approach advocated here is not like conventional methods of programming. Furthermore, the top-down approach is itself subject to several interpretations, some of which we disagree with. Top-down programming is discussed at length in Chapter 3. The following characteristics of the top-down approach are excerpts from that chapter.

1. *Design in Levels*. The programmer designs the program in *levels*, where a level consists of one or more modules. A module is always "complete," although it may reference unwritten submodules. The first level is a complete "main program." A lower level refines or develops unwritten modules in the upper level. In other words, the modules of a successive level consist of the submodules referenced in the prior level. The programmer may look several levels ahead to determine the best way to design the level at hand.

2. *Initial Language Independence*. The programmer initially uses expressions (often in English) that are relevant to the problem solution, even though the expressions cannot be directly transliterated into COBOL. From statements that are machine and language independent, the programmer moves toward a final machine implementation in COBOL.

3. *Postponement of Details to Lower Levels*. The programmer concentrates on critical broad issues at the initial levels and postpones details (for example, choice of specific algorithms or intermediate data representations) until lower levels.

4. *Formalization of Each Level*. Before proceeding to a lower level, the programmer ensures that the "program" in its current stage of development is a "formal" statement. In most cases this means a program that calls unwritten submodules with all arguments spelled out. This step insures that further sections of the program will be developed independently, without later changing the specifications or the interfaces between modules.

5. *Verification of Each Level*. After generating the modules of a new

**Example 2.3 P₁ (Informal) and P₁ (Formal) for the Payroll and
Report Program of Chap. 3**

P₁ (Informal): Produce ACM payroll and report

describe input and output files
open files and check labels
read a payroll record
read a work record
if either read attempt indicates an empty file
    then write appropriate message to system console
    else produce payroll and report
stop

P₁ (Formal): Produce ACM payroll and report

describe files (OLD-PAYROLL-MASTER-FILE, WORK-REC-FILE,
      NEW-PAYROLL-MASTER-FILE, OPERATIONS-BOARD-RPT,
      PAY-REC-FILE, ILLEGAL-WORK-REC-DECK)
open files and check labels OLD-PAYROLL-MASTER-FILE,
      WORK-REC-FILE.
read an EMPL-PAYROLL-REC from OLD-PAYROLL-MASTER-FILE
read an EMP-WORK-REC from WORK-REC-FILE.

select the appropriate action.
    if (OLD-PAYROLL-MASTER-FILE *and* WORK-REC-FILE are empty)
      then write program message to system console. (See condition 2.1
        in condition-action list)
    if (OLD-PAYROLL-MASTER-FILE is empty *but* WORK-REC-FILE is
      not empty)
      then write program message to system console. (See condition 2.2)
    if (OLD-PAYROLL-MASTER-FILE is not empty *but*
      WORK-REC-FILE is empty)
      then write program message to system console. (See condition 2.3)
    if (OLD-PAYROLL-MASTER-FILE *and* WORK-REC-FILE are not
      empty)
      then produce payroll and report
        —using for input EMPL-PAYROLL-REC,
          EMPL-WORK-REC, OLD-PAYROLL-MASTER-FILE,
          WORK-REC-FILE
        —possibly outputting PAY-REC-FILE, OPERATIONS-
          BOARD-RPT, NEW-PAYROLL-MASTER-FILE,
          ILLEGAL-WORK-REC-DECK (console messages)

close files OLD-PAYROLL-MASTER-FILE, WORK-REC-FILE
stop

---

level, the programmer verifies the developing formal statement of the program. This insures that errors pertinent to the current level of development will be detected at their own level.

6. *Successive Refinements*. Each level of the program is refined, formalized, and verified in successive levels until the programmer obtains the completed program that can be transformed easily into COBOL.

Consider Example 2.3, which gives the first level of the program for the payroll and report problem of Chapter 3. Examining the definition of the problem, the programmer writes a complete but informal main program P_1. After a somewhat more detailed look at the problem definition and considering the overall algorithm chosen earlier, the programmer develops P_1 into a formal version. The formal main program is in some sense complete and can be verified as if it had been written in an actual programming language. The module to produce a payroll and report referenced in P_1 must be written in P_2 and refined further in successive levels if necessary.

Top-down programming has two distinct advantages. First, it initially frees a programmer from the confines of COBOL and allows him to deal with more natural data structures or actions. Second, it leads to a structured modular approach that allows the programmer to write statements relevant to the current structures or actions. The details can be developed later in separate modules. In fact, the main goal of top-down programming is just that: to aid the programmer in writing well-structured, modular programs.

We cannot really say it all here. Chapter 3 tells the whole story.

Proverb 6 BEWARE OF OTHER APPROACHES

Traditionally, programmers have used many different approaches to a program. Consider the following list:

1. Bottom-up approach
2. Inside-out or forest approach
3. Linear approach
4. Typical systems analyst approach
5. Imitation approach

In the "bottom-up" approach, the programmer writes the lower modules first and the upper levels later. The bottom-up approach is in a sense the inversion of the top-down approach. It suffers severely by requiring the programmer to make specific decisions about the program before the overall problem and algorithm are understood.

In between the top-down and the bottom-up approaches, we have the "inside-out" or "forest" approach, which consists of starting in the middle of the program and working down and up at the same time. Roughly speaking, it goes as follows:

1. *General Idea.*   First we decide upon the general idea for programming the problem.
2. *A Rough Sketch of the Program.*   Next we write any "important" sections of the program, assuming initialization in some form. In some sections we write portions of the actual code. In doing this, we hope that the actual intent of each piece of code will not change several times, necessitating rewriting parts of our sketch.
3. *Coding the First Version.*   After Step 3, we write specific code for the entire program. We start with the lowest level module. After an individual module has been coded, we debug it and immediately prepare a description of what it does.
4. *Rethinking and Revising.*   As a result of Step 3, we should be close to a working program, but it may be possible to improve on it. So we continue by making several improvements until we obtain a complete working program.

We think it fair to say that many programmers work inside out. Usually they don't start very close to the top or bottom levels. Instead they start in the middle and work outwards until a program finally appears on the horizon. The approach is a poor one, for the program may undergo many changes and patches and thus seldom achieves a clear logical structure.

The third method is called the "linear" approach. Here, one immediately starts writing code as it will appear when executed: first line first, second line second, and so forth. The debit with this approach is the need to make specific detailed decisions with very little assurance that they are appropriate to the problem at hand. One must then accept the consequences. This technique may seem obviously poor, but the temptation to use it can be strong.

The fourth technique is the typical "systems analyst" approach. When used wisely it can be an effective technique, and admittedly it has been successfully used for many large programs. We shall briefly compare it to the top-down approach, the technique advocated in this book. The systems analyst often starts on a large programming problem by dividing up the task on the basis of the flow of control he sees in the overall program. The flowchart picturing the flow is broken into a number of modules, which are then farmed out to the programmers. After these have been completed, the analyst will firm up the interfaces and try to make things work right. The lower level modules receive attention before their function and data requirements are explicit. The resulting program modules are primarily determined by the flow of control through the program; thus the importance of flowcharts with this technique.

With the top-down approach, on the other hand, the flow of control is subservient to the logical structure. There does not have to be an identifiable flow of control that is easy to flowchart. The flow of control is rather like traversing a tree. It starts at the top level, goes down one or more levels, comes back, goes on to another level, and so forth. The top-down approach thus has little need for flowcharting.

As a final method, consider what we call the "imitation" approach, a method superficially resembling the top-down approach. This approach is discussed in detail because many programmers think that the top-down approach is really the way they have always programmed. We claim that there are often subtle but important differences. The imitation approach is described as follows:

1. *Thinking about the Program.* Having been given a programming assignment, take the time to examine the problem thoroughly before starting to program. Think about the details of the program for a while, and then decide on a general approach.

2. *Deciding on Submodules.* After having thought about the problem in detail, decide on what sections will be sufficiently important to merit being made into submodules.

3. *Data Representation.* After compiling a list of the submodules, decide on a data representation that will enable them to be efficient, unless the representation is already specified.

4. *Coding of Submodules.* At this point write each submodule. After each is completed, write down what it expects as input, what it returns as output, and what it does. The submodules should be written in a hierarchical manner: the most primitive first, calling routines second, and so forth. Doing this will insure that the submodules are fully coded before the upper-level program structures are finalized.

5. *Coding the Main Program.* After all submodules have been written, write the main program. The purpose of the main program will be sequencing and interfacing the subroutines.

The imitation approach has some important resemblances to the top-down approach: (1) The programmer must understand the problem thoroughly before writing code; (2) the actual writing of the program is postponed until after certain decisions have been made; and (3) the problem is broken up into logical units. However, there are important different characteristics in the two approaches.

1. In the top-down approach, a *specific* plan of attack is developed in stages. Only the issues relevant to a given level are considered, and these issues are formalized completely.

2. In the top-down approach, data representations are delayed as *long* as possible and then they are made to fit the algorithm rather than the other way around.

3. Furthermore, whenever the programmer decides to use a subprogram or procedure, the interfaces (that is, arguments, returned values, and effects) are decided *first*. The inputs and outputs are formalized before

developing the submodule; that is, the submodules are made to fit the calling routine instead of the other way around.

4. Most important, at *every step* in the top-down approach, the programmer must have a complete, correct "program."

The major disadvantages of the imitation approach are that it is more likely to produce errors, to require major program modifications, or to result in an unstructured COBOL program. Choosing a partially specified attack may require serious changes to the program. Coding submodules first may result in a confusing program logic if the submodules do not happen to integrate easily into upper level code designed later. Finally, early emphasis on data representation or program details may obscure an entirely better algorithm.

In summary, think carefully about programming technique. The top-down approach, which is discussed at length in Chapter 3, may provide a wise alternative.

Proverb 7   CODE IN LOGICAL UNITS

The best programs are those that can be understood easily. There are no superfluous details and the logical structure is clear. Such well-structured programs are always a by-product of a careful development process and are usually characterized by small, functionally specific modules. Generally, the statements of a COBOL module should not extend beyond one page.

The most direct value of modular code is felt during program maintenance, for time is not wasted trying to determine what is being done over several sections of code. Consider Fig. 2.3a, which outlines the logical structure of a hypothetical program. The structure is difficult to follow. Figure 2.3b pictures the remedied situation where simple computations are isolated in units.

There are many assets to modular code. Coding time is shortened by the use of previously written modules. Implementation costs are lower because of easier overlaying, decreased recompilation costs, smaller tasks, and isolated code bottlenecks. Testing is much simpler because of the fact that "simple" modules usually have no more than, say, a half dozen looping and branching constructs and thus a small number of total execution paths.

When the time comes to write actual COBOL code, there are three guidelines that will help you code in logical units:

1. First and most obviously, use the PERFORM and CALL statements.
2. Don't use the GO TO.
3. Prettyprint to display the resulting logical structure.

The next three proverbs treat these issues.

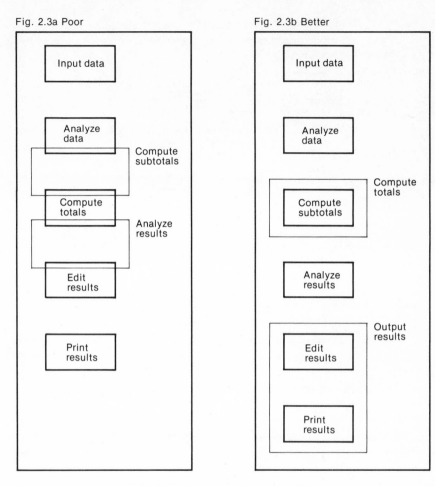

Fig. 2.3a Poor   Fig. 2.3b Better

Fig. 2.3   Display of logical structure

Proverb 8   USE PERFORM AND CALL

The procedure and subprogram facilities in COBOL can be powerful tools for coding clear, modular programs. Not only do these facilities allow the programmer to "factor out" frequently executed sections of code, but more importantly, they provide a basic unit for abstraction of program modules. This abstraction can have a great effect on program readability by exposing the program's logical structure.

Consider the Procedure Division in Example 2.4a. Despite the simple nature of the operations, the length and succession of details must have made

Example 2.4a   A "Monolithic" Procedure Division

```
PROCEDURE DIVISION.

    PREPARE-FOR-UPDATE.
       OPEN INPUT    SALE-TRANSACTION-FILE
            I-O      SALESPERSON-MASTER-FILE
            OUTPUT   PROGRAM-ACTION-RPT.
       MOVE 0 TO  NUM-OF-UPDATES,
                  NUM-OF-UNMATCHED-TRANSACTIONS.
       ACCEPT  TODAYS-DATE IN ACTION-RPT-HEADER  FROM DATE.
       WRITE  RPT-LINE  FROM  ACTION-RPT-HEADER
          AFTER ADVANCING PAGE.

    UPDATE-WITH-NEXT-TRANSACTION.
       READ  SALE-TRANSACTION-FILE
          AT END    GO TO  COMPLETE-ACTION-RPT.
       MOVE  SALESPERSON-ID-NUM IN TRANSACTION-REC
             TO  ID IN MASTER-REC.
       READ  SALESPERSON-MASTER-FILE
          INVALID KEY   GO TO  HANDLE-UNMATCHED-TRANSACTION.
       PERFORM  UPDATE-MASTER-REC.
       REWRITE  MASTER-REC
          INVALID KEY   GO TO  ABORT-PROGRAM.
       ADD 1 TO  NUM-OF-UPDATES.
       GO TO  UPDATE-WITH-NEXT-TRANSACTION.

    COMPLETE-ACTION-RPT.
       MOVE  NUM-OF-UNMATCHED-TRANSACTIONS
             TO  TOTAL-UNMATCHED IN TOTAL-UNMATCHED-LINE.
       WRITE  RPT-LINE  FROM  TOTAL-UNMATCHED-LINE
          AFTER ADVANCING 2 LINES.
       MOVE  NUM-OF-UPDATES
             TO  TOTAL-UPDATES IN TOTAL-UPDATES-LINE.
       WRITE  RPT-LINE  FROM TOTAL-UPDATES-LINE
          AFTER ADVANCING 3 LINES.
       MOVE SPACES TO  RPT-LINE.
       WRITE  RPT-LINE
          BEFORE ADVANCING PAGE.
       GO TO  CLEANUP-AFTER-UPDATE.

    HANDLE-UNMATCHED-TRANSACTION.
       IF (NUM-OF-UNMATCHED-TRANSACTIONS  =  0)
          WRITE  RPT-LINE  FROM  UNMATCH-LIST-HEADER
             AFTER ADVANCING 2 LINES.
       ADD 1 TO  NUM-OF-UNMATCHED-TRANSACTIONS.
       MOVE CORRESPONDING  TRANSACTION-REC
             TO  UNMATCHED-TRANSACTION-LINE.
       WRITE  RPT-LINE FROM  UNMATCHED-TRANSACTION-LINE.
       GO TO  UPDATE-WITH-NEXT-TRANSACTION.

    UPDATE-MASTER-REC.
       ...

    ABORT-PROGRAM.
       ...

    CLEANUP-AFTER-UPDATE.
       CLOSE  SALE-TRANSACTION-FILE,
              SALESPERSON-MASTER-FILE,
              PROGRAM-ACTION-RPT.
       STOP RUN.
```

coding a mental feat. Every time a line was coded, its relationship to the entire program had to be considered. When reading this program in hope of modifying it, one must first search through the maze of details to locate the area in need of

Example 2.4b   Effective Use of the Perform Statement

```
PROCEDURE DIVISION.


TOP-LEVEL  SECTION.

   MAIN-PROGRAM.
      OPEN INPUT    SALE-TRANSACTION-FILE
           I-O      SALESPERSON-MASTER-FILE
           OUTPUT   PROGRAM-ACTION-RPT.
      MOVE 0 TO  SALE-TRANSACTION-FILE-STATUS,
                 PROGRAM-ABORT-STATUS.
      MOVE 0 TO  NUM-OF-UPDATES,
                 NUM-OF-UNMATCHED-TRANSACTIONS.
      PERFORM  PREPARE-ACTION-RPT.
      PERFORM  INCORPORATE-NEXT-TRANSACTION
         UNTIL (EOF-SALE-TRANSACTION-FILE  OR  PROGRAM-ABORT).
      PERFORM  COMPLETE-ACTION-RPT.
      CLOSE  SALE-TRANSACTION-FILE,
             SALESPERSON-MASTER-FILE,
             PROGRAM-ACTION-RPT.
      STOP RUN.


LEVEL-2-ROUTINES  SECTION.

   PREPARE-ACTION-RPT.
      PERFORM  PRODUCE-PAGE-EJECT.
      PERFORM  PRODUCE-ACTION-RPT-HEADER.

   INCORPORATE-NEXT-TRANSACTION.
      PERFORM  GET-NEXT-TRANSACTION-REC.
      IF (NOT  EOF-SALE-TRANSACTION-FILE)
        PERFORM  GET-MATCHING-MASTER-REC
        IF (MATCHING-MASTER-REC-OBTAINED)
           PERFORM  UPDATE-MASTER-REC
           ADD 1 TO  NUM-OF-UPDATES
           PERFORM  REFILE-MASTER-REC
           IF (REFILE-FAILED)
              MOVE 1 TO  PROGRAM-ABORT-STATUS
           ELSE
              NEXT SENTENCE
        ELSE
           PERFORM  HANDLE-UNMATCHED-TRANSACTION
           ADD 1 TO  NUM-UNMATCHED-TRANSACTIONS.

   COMPLETE-ACTION-RPT.
      IF (PROGRAM-ABORT)
         ...

      ELSE
         PERFORM  PRODUCE-LINE-SKIP
         PERFORM  PRODUCE-UNMATCH-SUMMARY
         PERFORM  PRODUCE-LINE-SKIP  2  TIMES
         PERFORM  PRODUCE-UPDATE-SUMMARY
         PERFORM  PRODUCE-PAGE-EJECT.


LEVEL-3-ROUTINES  SECTION.

   UPDATE-MASTER-REC.
      ...

   HANDLE-UNMATCHED-TRANSACTION.
      IF (NUM-OF-UNMATCHED-TRANSACTIONS  =  0)
         PERFORM  PRODUCE-LINE-SKIP
         PERFORM  PRODUCE-UNMATCH-LIST-HEADER.
      PERFORM  LIST-UNMATCHED-TRANSACTION.
```

Example 2.4b (cont'd)

```
I-O-ROUTINES  SECTION.

    PRODUCE-PAGE-EJECT.
        MOVE SPACES TO  RPT-LINE.
        WRITE  RPT-LINE
            BEFORE ADVANCING PAGE.

    PRODUCE-ACTION-RPT-HEADER.
        ACCEPT TODAYS-DATE IN ACTION-RPT-HEADER
            FROM DATE.
        MOVE  ACTION-RPT-HEADER  TO  RPT-LINE.
        PERFORM  FREE-RPT-LINE.

    GET-NEXT-TRANSACTION-REC.
        READ  SALE-TRANSACTION-FILE
            AT END     MOVE 1 TO  SALE-TRANSACTION-FILE-STATUS.

    GET-MATCHING-MASTER-REC.
        MOVE  SALESPERSON-ID-NUM IN TRANSACTION-REC
                TO  ID IN MASTER-REC.
        MOVE 0 TO  MATCHING-MASTER-REC-STATUS.
        READ  SALESPERSON-MASTER-FILE
            INVALID KEY     MOVE 1 TO  MATCHING-MASTER-REC-STATUS.

    REFILE-MASTER-REC.
        MOVE  SALESPERSON-ID-NUM IN TRANSACTION-REC
        MOVE  SALESPERSON-ID-NUM IN TRANSACTION-REC
                TO  ID IN MASTER-REC.
        MOVE 0 TO  REFILE-STATUS.
        REWRITE  MASTER-REC
            INVALID KEY      MOVE 1 TO  REFILE-STATUS.

    PRODUCE-LINE-SKIP.
        MOVE SPACES TO  RPT-LINE.
        PERFORM  FREE-RPT-LINE.

    PRODUCE-UNMATCH-SUMMARY.
        MOVE  NUM-OF-UNMATCHED-TRANSACTIONS
                TO  TOTAL-UNMATCHED IN TOTAL-UNMATCHED-LINE.
        MOVE  TOTAL-UNMATCHED-LINE  TO  RPT-LINE.
        PERFORM  FREE-RPT-LINE.

    PRODUCE-UPDATE-SUMMARY.
        MOVE  NUM-OF-UPDATES
                TO  TOTAL-UPDATES IN TOTAL-UPDATES-LINE.
        MOVE  TOTAL-UPDATES-LINE  TO  RPT-LINE.
        PERFORM  FREE-RPT-LINE.

    PRODUCE-UNMATCH-LIST-HEADER.
        MOVE  UNMATCH-LIST-HEADER  TO  RPT-LINE.
        PERFORM  FREE-RPT-LINE.

    LIST-UNMATCHED-TRANSACTION.
        MOVE CORRESPONDING  TRANSACTION-REC
                TO  UNMATCHED-TRANSACTION-LINE.
        MOVE  UNMATCHED-TRANSACTION-LINE  TO  RPT-LINE.
        PERFORM  FREE-RPT-LINE.

    FREE-RPT-LINE.
        WRITE  RPT-LINE
            BEFORE ADVANCING 1 LINE.
```

change and then consider the impact on the entire program of every line changed or added. Such is the case with a "monolithic" structured program [Ref. Z2] .

A clearly better program that results when one starts anew (see Proverb

Example 2.5   How General Use Subroutines Should Be Called

```
EXAMPLE 2.5A   POOR


        PRODUCE-ACTION-RPT-HEADER.
         ACCEPT  TODAYS-DATE  FROM DATE.
         PERFORM  CALCULATE-JULIAN-DAY.
         MOVE  JULIAN-DAY
               TO  EDITED-JULIAN-DAY IN ACTION-RPT-HEADER.
         ...


EXAMPLE 2.5B   BETTER


        PRODUCE-ACTION-RPT-HEADER.
         CALL  "CALCULATE-JULIAN-DAY"
          USING JULIAN-DAY.
         CANCEL  "CALCULATE-JULIAN-DAY".
         MOVE  JULIAN-DAY
               TO  EDITED-JULIAN-DAY IN ACTION-RPT-HEADER.
         ...
```

19) is given in Example 2.4b. Here, the PERFORM statement is used to advantage by suppressing needless details and isolating functions in levels. Notably, modules have a comprehensible size. Coding and code reading need not be involved with the total program at every turn.

Let us now suppose that you have nearly completed the coding of Example 2.4b. You are notified of a design change that requires the Julian day to be printed in the action report header. You should not respond to this change by writing and performing the paragraph CALCULATE-JULIAN-DAY as in Example 2.5a.

One can PERFORM those subroutines which are "problem specific" but should CALL those which could be valuable in other programs. The subroutine CALCULATE-JULIAN-DAY should be isolated neatly from the procedure division by coding it as a subprogram that can be simply called as in Example 2.5b. If you are lucky, someone else might have already written a program that yields the Julian day.

In brief, use procedures and subprograms. They can make the program much easier to understand and maintain.

Proverb 9   DON'T GO TO

All procedure-oriented programming languages have the notion of "control flow," which is the trace of basic actions in a program. Besides the control flow to the next sequential statement, control flow is specified by explicit "control structures" or "control statements." For example, in COBOL we have, among others, the IF, PERFORM, and GO TO control statements. As pointed out in

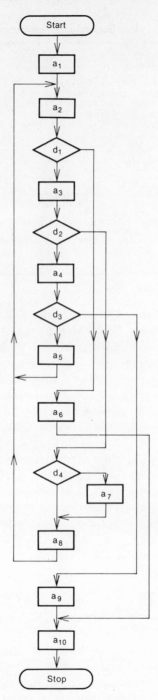

Fig. 2.4   Schematic flow of control in Example 2.4a.

Reference L3, the basic function of a control structure is to clarify operational abstraction.

Unfortunately, the use of the GO TO statement by itself (and more so in the context of other GO TOs) can easily destroy good operational abstraction by forcing the reader to follow control paths around a program. We believe that the GO TO statement is more than just a poor control structure. Its involvement with needless detail and with visual jumping makes it a construct to be avoided.

While most people will agree that the GO TO statement provides no operational abstraction, many argue for its continued use because of its execution efficiency. In truth, however, this is but "micro-efficiency," which we caution against in Chapter 5. Before considering optimizations based on the use of the GO TO, a programmer should be concerned with "macro-efficient" optimizations such as choosing a more appropriate file structure, using a good optimizing compiler, or replacing a linear table search with a binary one. In cases where efficiency requirements are very strict, the programmer still should not rely on GO TOs but should consider assembly languages where much larger gains can be made. The reader who wishes a comprehensive discussion of the case against the GO TO is referred to Reference L3.

Consider Example 2.4a of the previous proverb, a simple main program entangled by GO TOs. You don't read this module; you figure it out. To avoid coding GO TOs, one must employ a good approach to programming and use other control verbs, notably the IF, CALL and PERFORM verbs. As an alternative to this main program, consider Example 2.4b, which resulted from a careful top-down approach to the program.

The diagram in Fig. 2.4 helps one appreciate the effect of the GO TO on a module's logical structure. This schema exhibits the flow of control that the reader sees within the program text of Example 2.4a. In Example 2.4b, on the other hand, control passes down and back up a tree structure and is sequential for all modules at all levels.

There are many techniques for utilizing the IF, CALL, and PERFORM verbs instead of the GO TO. Table 2.2 lists a few salient ones. There are others, and eventually you should add them to your repertoire.

In short, forget about the GO TO. In time, after using other simple control structures, you will never miss it.

Proverb 10 PRETTYPRINT

If there is one proverb that is simple to follow but enormously effective, this is it. Briefly stated, "prettyprinting" is the effective utilization of "extra" spaces, blank lines, or special characters to illuminate the logical structure of a program. The COBOL language allows a generous use of blank spaces and lines to promote prettyprinting.

Table 2.2   Alternatives to the GO TO

ALTERATION OF A CONDITIONAL EXPRESSION

(A)   IF (NUM-OF-UNMATCHED-TRANSACTIONS NOT EQUAL ZERO)
            GO TO LIST-TRANSACTION.
         PERFORM PRODUCE-LINE-SKIP.
         PERFORM PRODUCE-UNMATCH-LIST-HEADER.

         LIST-TRANSACTION.
         PERFORM LIST-UNMATCHED-TRANSACTION.

(B)   IF (NUM-OF-UNMATCHED-TRANSACTIONS EQUAL ZERO)
            PERFORM PRODUCE-LINE-SKIP
            PERFORM PRODUCE-UNMATCHED-LIST-HEADER.
         PERFORM LIST-UNMATCHED-TRANSACTION.

USE OF A SIMPLE PERFORM STATEMENT

(A)   READ CUSTOMER-ORDERS-FILE
            AT END   GO TO NOTHING-TO-DO.
         ...

         NOTHING-TO-DO.
         PERFORM PRODUCE-PAGE-EJECT.
         PERFORM PRODUCE-NO-ORDERS-MESSAGE.
         CLOSE CUSTOMER-ORDERS-FILE,
                SALES-RPT.
         STOP RUN.

(B)   PERFORM GET-NEXT-ORDER-REC.
         IF (EMPTY-CUSTOMER-ORDERS-FILE)
            PERFORM PRODUCE-PAGE-EJECT
            PERFORM PRODUCE-NO-ORDERS-MESSAGE
         ELSE
            ...

         CLOSE CUSTOMER-ORDERS-FILE,
                SALES-RPT.
         STOP RUN.

USE OF A PERFORM-UNTIL STATEMENT

(A)   PROCESS-NEXT-ORDER-REC.
         READ CUSTOMER-ORDERS-FILE
            AT END GO TO PRODUCE-ACTION-RPT.
         ...

         GO TO PROCESS-NEXT-ORDER-REC.

(B)   PERFORM PROCESS-NEXT-ORDER-REC
            UNTIL (EOF-CUSTOMER-ORDERS-FILE).
         PERFORM PRODUCE-ACTION-RPT.

Table 2.2 (cont'd)

```
USE OF PERFORM-VARYING-UNTIL OR SEARCH STATEMENTS


 (A)      VALIDATE-JOB-ID-NUM.
          MOVE 1 TO  DESCRIPTION-SUBSCRIPT.

          SEARCH-JOB-DESCRIPTION-TABLE.
          IF (DESCRIPTION-SUBSCRIPT  >  SIZE-JOB-DESCRIPTION-TABLE)
             MOVE "*"  TO CONTRACT-REC-ERROR-LOG (3)
             GO TO  VALIDATE-NUM-EMPLOYED.
          IF (JOB-ID-NUM  =  ID-NUM (DESCPIPTION-SUBSCRIPT))
             MOVE SPACE TO  CONTRACT-REC-ERROR-LOG (3)
             GO TO  VALIDATE-NUM-EMPLOYED.
          ADD 1 TO  DESCRIPTION-SUBSCRIPT.
          GO TO  SEARCH-JOB-DESCRIPTION-TABLE.


 (B)      VALIDATE-JOB-ID-NUM.
          MOVE 0 TO  SEARCH-CONDITION.
          PERFORM  SEARCH-JOB-DESCRIPTION-TABLE
                   VARYING  DESCRIPTION-SUBSCRIPT  FROM 1 BY 1
                   UNTIL (DESCRIPTION-FOUND  OR  NO-DESCRIPTION-EXISTS).
          IF (DESCRIPTION-FOUND)
             MOVE SPACE TO  CONTRACT-REC-ERROR-LOG (3)
          ELSE
             MOVE "*" TO  CONTRACT-REC-ERROR-LOG (3).


 (C)      VALIDATE-JOB-ID-NUM.
          SET DESCRIPTION-INDEX  TO 1.
          SEARCH  JOB-DESCRIPTION
             AT END
                    MOVE "*" TO  CONTRACT-REC-ERROR-LOG (3)
             WHEN (ID-NUM (DESCRIPTION-INDEX)  =  JOB-ID-NUM)
                    MOVE SPACE TO  CONTRACT-REC-ERROR-LOG (3).
```

Prettyprinting is especially important in the verification and maintenance of programs. With good prettyprinting it is fairly easy to detect errors, such as improperly structured data description entries and incorrectly nested IF statements. Furthermore, a programmer trying to read the program does not have to devote extra time to discovering its structure, an advantage that can greatly reduce the difficulty in understanding the program.

Consider the programs of Example 2.6, two deck reproducing routines that place sequence numbers and identification tags on the cards of a COBOL source deck. The program of Example 2.6a is typically produced by a programmer who does not give much thought to prettyprinting. Example 2.6b shows how great an improvement is made when careful prettyprinting is applied. (Note that in most installations the use of the Report Writer for such simple programs takes considerable storage space.)

One objection to prettyprinting is the initial extra effort required. However, with a good text editor or with judicious use of program drum cards, the effort can be reduced significantly. Unfortunately, a COBOL programmer must be aware of "Sequence Number Area," "Indicator Area," "Area A," and "Area

Example 2.6a   Token Thought Given to Prettyprinting

```
IDENTIFICATION DIVISION.
PROGRAM-ID.  REPRODUCE-COBOL-SOURCE-DECK.

AUTHOR.  GAIL A. MICHAEL,     TEL (617) 271-2234.

INSTALLATION.  LEE CORPORATION,  STONEHAM, MA.

DATE-COMPILED.  75 FEB 22.

SECURITY.  NO CHECK IS MADE TO INSURE THAT THE INPUT DECK CONTAINS
           FEWER THAN 100,000 CARDS.

*          FOR INPUT, THIS PROGRAM EXPECTS A COBOL SOURCE PROGRAM
*      CARD WITH THE FOLLOWING INFORMATION:
*          COLUMN 1 = "*"
*          COLUMNS 2-9 = PROGRAM IDENTIFICATION FIELD
*      AS NORMAL OUTPUT, THIS PROGRAM PRODUCES AN UPDATED
*      COPY OF THE INPUT DECK AND A PRINTED LISTING OF THE
*      UPDATED COPY.  EACH CARD OF THE UPDATED COPY IS GIVEN A
*      NEW SEQUENCE NUMBER AND THE NEW PROGRAM IDENTIFICATION.
*      SEQUENCE NUMBERS START WITH 000010 AND INCREASE BY
*      10 ON EACH SUCCESSIVE CARD.
*          AS ABNORMAL OUTPUT, THIS PROGRAM PRODUCES A PRINTED
*       REPORT OF ENCOUNTERED ERRORS.

ENVIRONMENT DIVISION.
CONFIGURATION SECTION.

SOURCE-COMPUTER.  UNIVERSAL-6.
OBJECT COMPUTER.  UNIVERSAL-6.

INPUT-OUTPUT  SECTION.
FILE-CONTROL.
    SELECT  INPUT-DECK
    ASSIGN TO  CARD-RDR-X17.
    SELECT  NEW-SOURCE-DECK
    ASSIGN TO  CARD-PCH-01.
    SELECT  REPORT-FILE
    ASSIGN TO  LINE-PTR-Y7.

DATA DIVISION.

FILE SECTION.
FD  INPUT-DECK
    RECORD CONTAINS 80 CHARACTERS
    LABEL RECORDS OMITTED.
01  CONTROL-CARD.
    02 MARKER          PIC X(1).
    02 NEW-PROGRAM-ID  PIC X(8).
    02 FILLER          PIC X(71).
01  OLD-SOURCE-CARD.
    02 FILLER             PIC X(6).
    02 INDICATOR-A-B-AREAS  PIC X(66).
    02 FILLER             PIC X(8).

FD  NEW-SOURCE-DECK
    RECORD CONTAINS 80 CHARACTERS
    LABEL RECORDS OMITTED.
01  NEW-SOURCE-CARD.
    02 SEQUENCE-NUM-AREA  PIC 9(6).
    02 INDICATOR-A-B-AREAS  PIC X(66).
    02 PROGRAM-ID-AREA   PIC X(8).
FD  REPORT-FILE
    RECORD CONTAINS 120 CHARACTERS
    LABEL RECORDS OMITTED
    REPORTS ARE  DECK-LISTING-RPT  PROGRAM-ABORT-RPT.
```

Example 2.6a (cont'd)

```
WORKING-STORAGE  SECTION.
01  INPUT-DATA-ITEMS.
    02 EXPECTED-CONTROL-CARD-MARKER   PIC X(1)  VALUE "*".
    02 INPUT-DECK-CONDITION           PIC 9(1).
       88 EOF-INPUT-DECK  VALUE 1.
       88 CONTROL-CARD-ERROR  VALUE 2.
01  OUTPUT-DATA-ITEMS.
    02 ERROR-OCCURRENCE           PIC X(100).
    02 ERROR-MESSAGES.
       03 MISSING-INPUT-DECK-MESSAGE        PIC X(100),
          VALUE "INPUT DECK IS MISSING.".
       03 MISSING-CONTROL-CARD-MESSAGE      PIC X(100),  VALUE
          "CONTROL CARD HEADING INPUT DECK IS MISSING.".
    02 NEW-PROGRAM-ID           PIC X(8).
    02 NEW-SEQUENCE-NUM          PIC 9(6).
    02 TODAYS-DATE              PIC 9(6).



REPORT  SECTION.
RD  DECK-LISTING-RPT
    PAGE 66 LINES  HEADING 4  FIRST DETAIL 8
    LAST DETAIL 63.
01  TYPE PAGE HEADING,  LINE 4.
    02 COLUMN 10  PIC X(30)  VALUE
       "REPRODUCE-COBOL-SOURCE-DECK".
    02 COLUMN 50  PIC 9(2)/9(2)/9(2)  SOURCE  IS TODAYS-DATE.
    02 COLUMN 90  PIC X(5)  VALUE  "PAGE:".
    02 COLUMN 96  PIC Z(5)9  SOURCE IS  PAGE-COUNTER.
01  NEW-SOURCE-CARD-LINE   TYPE DETAIL,  LINE PLUS 1.
    02 COLUMN 1  PIC 9(6),
       SOURCE IS  NEW-SEQUENCE-NUM IN OUTPUT-DATA-ITEMS.
    02 COLUMN 7  PIC X(66),
       SOURCE IS  INDICATOR-A-B-AREAS IN OLD-SOURCE-CARD.
    02 COLUMN 73  PIC X(8),
       SOURCE IS  NEW-PROGRAM-ID IN OUTPUT-DATA-ITEMS.

RD  PROGRAM-ABORT-RPT
    PAGE 66 LINES  HEADING 4  FIRST DETAIL 8
    LAST DETAIL 63.

01  TYPE PAGE HEADING,  LINE 4.
    02 COLUMN 10,  PIC X(30),  VALUE
       "REPRODUCE-COBOL-SOURCE-DECK".
    02 COLUMN 50,  PIC 9(2)/9(2)/9(2),  SOURCE IS  TODAYS-DATE.
    02 COLUMN 90,  PIC X(5),  VALUE "PAGE:".
    02 COLUMN 96,  PIC X(5)9,           SOURCE IS  PAGE-COUNTER.

01  ABORT-MESSAGE  TYPE DETAIL,  LINE PLUS 1.
    02 COLUMN 1,  PIC X(10),  VALUE "*** ERROR:".
    02 COLUMN 12,  PIC X(100),  SOURCE IS  ERROR-OCCURRENCE.



PROCEDURE DIVISION.
TOP-LEVEL  SECTION.
MAIN-PROGRAM.
    OPEN INPUT   INPUT-DECK
         OUTPUT REPORT-FILE.
    MOVE 0 TO  INPUT-DECK-CONDITION.
    ACCEPT  TODAYS-DATE IN OUTPUT-DATA-ITEMS  FROM DATE.
    PERFORM  PROCESS-CONTROL-CARD.
    IF  (CONTROL-CARD-ERROR)
      INITIATE  PROGRAM-ABORT-RPT  GENERATE  ABORT-MESSAGE
      TERMINATE  PROGRAM-ABORT-RPT
      ELSE
```

Example 2.6a (cont'd)

```
                OPEN OUTPUT NEW-SOURCE-DECK
                INITIATE DECK-LISTING-RPT
                MOVE 0 TO NEW-SEQUENCE-NUM  IN OUTPUT-DATA-ITEMS
                PERFORM REDO-AND-LIST-NEXT-OLD-CARD
                UNTIL (EOF-INPUT-DECK)
                TERMINATE  DECK-LISTING-RPT
                CLOSE  NEW-SOURCE-DECK.
            CLOSE  INPUT-DECK, REPORT-FILE.  STOP RUN.

LEVEL-2-ROUTINES SECTION.
PROCESS-CONTROL-CARD.
     PERFORM  GET-NEXT-INPUT-CARD.
     IF (EOF-INPUT-DECK)
       MOVE 2 TO  INPUT-DECK-CONDITION
       MOVE  MISSING-INPUT-DECK-MESSAGE  TO  ERROR-OCCURRENCE
     ELSE
       IF (MARKER IN CONTROL-CARD  NOT EQUAL
         EXPECTED-CONTROL-CARD-MARKER)
         MOVE 2 TO  INPUT-DECK-CONDITION
         MOVE  MISSING-CONTROL-CARD-MESSAGE  TO  ERROR-OCCURRENCE
       ELSE
           MOVE  NEW-PROGRAM-ID IN CONTROL-CARD
           TO  NEW PROGRAM-ID IN OUTPUT-DATA-ITEMS.

REDO-AND-LIST-NEXT-OLD-CARD.
     PERFORM  GET-NEXT-INPUT-CARD.
     IF (NOT  EOF-INPUT-DECK)
       PERFORM  PRODUCE-NEW-SOURCE-CARD
       GENERATE  NEW-SOURCE-CARD-LINE.

I-O-ROUTINES  SECTION.
GET-NEXT-INPUT-CARD.
     READ  INPUT-DECK  AT END
     MOVE 1 TO  INPUT-DECK-CONDITION.
PRODUCE-NEW-SOURCE-CARD.
     MOVE  INDICATOR-A-B-AREAS IN OLD-SOURCE-CARD
     TO  INDICATOR-A-B-AREAS IN NEW-SOURCE-CARD.
     MOVE  NEW-PROGRAM-ID IN OUTPUT-DATA-ITEMS
     TO  PROGRAM-ID-AREA IN NEW-SOURCE-CARD.
     ADD 10 TO  NEW-SEQUENCE-NUM IN OUTPUT-DATA-ITEMS.
     MOVE  NEW-SEQUENCE-NUM IN OUTPUT-DATA-ITEMS
     TO  SEQUENCE-NUM-AREA IN NEW-SOURCE-CARD.
     WRITE  NEW-SOURCE-CARD.
```

Example 2.6b   Use of Good Prettyprinting Standards

```
IDENTIFICATION DIVISION.

  PROGRAM-ID.
    REPRODUCE-COBOL-SOURCE-DECK.

  AUTHOR.
    GAIL A. MICHAEL,     TEL (617) 271-2234.

  INSTALLATION.
    LEE CORPORATION,  STONEHAM, MA.

  DATE-COMPILED.
    75 FEB 22.

  SECURITY.
        NO CHECK IS MADE TO INSURE THAT THE INPUT DECK CONTAINS
        FEWER THAN 100,000 CARDS.
```

```
*     **    FOR INPUT, THIS PROGRAM EXPECTS A COBOL SOURCE PROGRAM
*     **  DECK OF FEWER THAN 100,000 CARDS PRECEDED BY A CONTROL
*     **  CARD WITH THE FOLLOWING INFORMATION:
*     **     COLUMN 1 = "*"
*     **     COLUMNS 2-9 = PROGRAM IDENTIFICATION FIELD
*     **
*     **    AS NORMAL OUTPUT, THIS PROGRAM PRODUCES AN UPDATED
*     **  COPY OF THE INPUT DECK AND A PRINTED LISTING OF THE
*     **  UPDATED COPY. EACH CARD OF THE UPDATED COPY IS GIVEN A
*     **  NEW SEQUENCE NUMBER AND THE NEW PROGRAM IDENTIFICATION.
*     **  SEQUENCE NUMBERS START WITH 000010 AND INCREASE BY
*     **  10 ON EACH SUCCESSIVE CARD.
*     **
*     **    AS ABNORMAL OUTPUT, THIS PROGRAM PRODUCES A PRINTED
*     **  REPORT OF ENCOUNTERED ERRORS.


ENVIRONMENT DIVISION.


CONFIGURATION SECTION.

   SOURCE-COMPUTER.
     UNIVERSAL-6.

   OBJECT COMPUTER.
     UNIVERSAL-6.


INPUT-OUTPUT SECTION.

   FILE-CONTROL.
     SELECT INPUT-DECK
       ASSIGN TO CARD-RDR-X17.
     SELECT NEW-SOURCE-DECK
       ASSIGN TO CARD-PCH-C1.
     SELECT REPORT-FILE
       ASSIGN TO LINE-PTR-YZ.



DATA DIVISION.


FILE SECTION.

   FD INPUT-DECK
       RECORD CONTAINS 80 CHARACTERS,
       LABEL RECORDS OMITTED.
   01 CONTROL-CARD.
     02 MARKER          PIC X(1).
     02 NEW-PROGRAM-ID  PIC X(8).
     02 FILLER          PIC X(71).
   01 OLD-SOURCE-CARD.
     02 FILLER             PIC X(6).
     02 INDICATOR-A-B-AREAS PIC X(66).
     02 FILLER             PIC X(8).

   FD NEW-SOURCE-DECK
       RECORD CONTAINS 80 CHARACTERS,
       LABEL RECORDS OMITTED.
   01 NEW-SOURCE-CARD.
     02 SEQUENCE-NUM-AREA   PIC 9(6).
     02 INDICATOR-A-B-AREAS PIC X(66).
     02 PROGRAM-ID-AREA     PIC X(8).
```

Example 2.6b (cont'd)

```
FD REPORT-FILE
      RECORD CONTAINS 120 CHARACTERS,
      LABEL RECORDS OMITTED,
      REPORTS ARE  DECK-LISTING-RPT,  PROGRAM-ABORT-RPT.



WORKING-STORAGE  SECTION.
   01  INPUT-DATA-ITEMS.
      02 EXPECTED-CONTROL-CARD-MARKER    PIC X(1),  VALUE "*".
      02 INPUT-DECK-CONDITION            PIC 9(1).
         88 EOF-INPUT-DECK                  VALUE 1.
         88 CONTROL-CARD-ERROR              VALUE 2.

   01  OUTPUT-DATA-ITEMS.
      02 ERROR-OCCURRENCE         PIC X(100).
      02 ERROR-MESSAGES.
         03 MISSING-INPUT-DECK-MESSAGE        PIC X(100),
            VALUE "INPUT DECK IS MISSING.".
         03 MISSING-CONTROL-CARD-MESSAGE      PIC X(100),
            VALUE "CONTROL CARD HEADING INPUT DECK IS MISSING.".
      02 NEW-PROGRAM-ID           PIC X(8).
      02 NEW-SEQUENCE-NUM         PIC 9(6).
      02 TODAYS-DATE              PIC 9(6).




REPORT  SECTION.

   RD DECK-LISTING-RPT
         PAGE 66 LINES,  HEADING 4,
            FIRST DETAIL 8, LAST DETAIL 63.

   01 TYPE PAGE HEADING,  LINE 4.
      02 COLUMN 10,  PIC X(30),
         VALUE "REPRODUCE-COBOL-SOURCE-DECK".
      02 COLUMN 50,  PIC 9(2)/9(2)/9(2),  SOURCE IS  TODAYS-DATE.
      02 COLUMN 90,  PIC X(5),  VALUE "PAGE:".
      02 COLUMN 96,  PIC Z(5)9,  SOURCE IS  PAGE-COUNTER.

   01 NEW-SOURCE-CARD-LINE   TYPE DETAIL,  LINE PLUS 1.
      02 COLUMN 1,  PIC 9(6),
            SOURCE IS  NEW-SEQUENCE-NUM IN OUTPUT-DATA-ITEMS.
      02 COLUMN 7, PIC X(66),
            SOURCE IS  INDICATOR-A-B-AREAS IN OLD-SOURCE-CARD.
      02 COLUMN 73, PIC X(8),
            SOURCE IS  NEW-PROGRAM-ID IN OUTPUT-DATA-ITEMS.


   RD PROGRAM-ABORT-RPT
         PAGE 66 LINES,  HEADING 4,
            FIRST DETAIL 8, LAST DETAIL 63.

   01 TYPE PAGE HEADING,  LINE 4.
      02 COLUMN 10,  PIC X(30),
         VALUE "REPRODUCE-COBOL-SOURCE-DECK".
      02 COLUMN 50,  PIC 9(2)/9(2)/9(2),  SOURCE IS  TODAYS-DATE.
      02 COLUMN 90,  PIC X(5),  VALUE "PAGE:".
      02 COLUMN 96,  PIC Z(5)9,
         SOURCE IS  PAGE-COUNTER.

   01 ABORT-MESSAGE   TYPE DETAIL,  LINE PLUS 1.
      02 COLUMN 1,  PIC X(10),       VALUE "*** ERROR:".
      02 COLUMN 12,  PIC X(100),      SOURCE IS  ERROR-OCCURRENCE.
```

Example 2.6b (cont'd)

```
PROCEDURE DIVISION.


TOP-LEVEL  SECTION.

  MAIN-PROGRAM.
    OPEN INPUT   INPUT-DECK
         OUTPUT REPORT-FILE.
    MOVE 0 TO  INPUT-DECK-CONDITION.
    ACCEPT  TODAYS-DATE IN OUTPUT-DATA-ITEMS  FROM DATE.
    PERFORM  PROCESS-CONTROL-CARD.
    IF (CONTROL-CARD-ERROR)
        INITIATE  PROGRAM-ABORT-RPT
        GENERATE  ABORT-MESSAGE
        TERMINATE  PROGRAM-ABORT-RPT
    ELSE
        OPEN OUTPUT  NEW-SOURCE-DECK
        INITIATE  DECK-LISTING-RPT
        MOVE 0 TO  NEW-SEQUENCE-NUM IN OUTPUT-DATA-ITEMS
        PERFORM  REDO-AND-LIST-NEXT-OLD-CARD
           UNTIL (EOF-INPUT-DECK)
        TERMINATE  DECK-LISTING-RPT
        CLOSE  NEW-SOURCE-DECK.
    CLOSE INPUT-DECK,  REPORT-FILE.
    STOP RUN.


LEVEL-2-ROUTINES  SECTION.

  PROCESS-CONTROL-CARD.
    PERFORM  GET-NEXT-INPUT-CARD.
    IF (EOF-INPUT-DECK)
      MOVE 2 TO  INPUT-DECK-CONDITION
      MOVE  MISSING-INPUT-DECK-MESSAGE  TO  ERROR-OCCURRENCE
    ELSE
      IF (MARKER IN CONTROL-CARD  NOT EQUAL
                       EXPECTED-CONTROL-CARD-MARKER)
        MOVE 2 TO  INPUT-DECK-CONDITION
        MOVE  MISSING-CONTROL-CARD-MESSAGE  TO  ERROR-OCCURRENCE
      ELSE
        MOVE  NEW-PROGRAM-ID IN CONTROL-CARD
              TO  NEW PROGRAM-ID IN OUTPUT-DATA-ITEMS.

  REDO-AND-LIST-NEXT-OLD-CARD.
    PERFORM  GET-NEXT-INPUT-CARD.
    IF (NOT  EOF-INPUT-DECK)
      PERFORM  PRODUCE-NEW-SOURCE-CARD
      GENERATE  NEW-SOURCE-CARD-LINE.


I-O-ROUTINES  SECTION.

  GET-NEXT-INPUT-CARD.
    READ  INPUT-DECK
      AT END   MOVE 1 TO  INPUT-DECK-CONDITION.

  PRODUCE-NEW-SOURCE-CARD.
    MOVE  INDICATOR-A-B-AREAS IN OLD-SOURCE-CARD.
          TO  INDICATOR-A-B-AREAS IN NEW-SOURCE-CARD.
    MOVE  NEW-PROGRAM-ID IN OUTPUT-DATA-ITEMS
          TO  PROGRAM-ID-AREA IN NEW-SOURCE-CARD.
    ADD 10 TO  NEW-SEQUENCE-NUM IN OUTPUT-DATA-ITEMS.
    MOVE  NEW-SEQUENCE-NUM IN OUTPUT-DATA-ITEMS
          TO  SEQUENCE-NUM-AREA IN NEW-SOURCE-CARD.
    WRITE  NEW-SOURCE-CARD.
```

B" for allowable program spacing. However, a little observation shows that most of the code writing occurs in Area B, where one can freely use multiple spaces and lines.

In all our examples, we have attempted to incorporate certain prettyprinting standards. The Appendix itemizes most of these standards. These rules are the product of many revisions and should be useful to all COBOL programmers. We encourage the reader to make use of additional prettyprinting standards as they are discovered. But do not hesitate to use the standards as they stand. If the program you are writing has a good logical structure, then show it!

Proverb 11   COMMENT EFFECTIVELY

COBOL allows two varieties of comments. The first consists of the comments within the Identification Division. The AUTHOR paragraph should always be present and should contain at least your full name. The SECURITY paragraph should contain a list of required forms and tapes, conditions for the authorization of users of the program, Save-Restart procedures, and other security issues pertinent to the given installation. Regular comment lines should be given immediately after the SECURITY paragraph. These should give a brief description of the program's intent, a reference to any special algorithms or conventions, and other pertinent general information.

The second variety of COBOL comments consists of comment lines within the program text. These comments should call attention only to issues not apparent in the code alone. These comments should point out abnormal cases, unusual side effects caused by procedures, particular algorithms used, and any other special notes.

There is considerable controversy over the proper use of comment lines in COBOL. As for the first variety of comments, some believe that external documentation is the better choice and that the Identification Division therefore requires only sparse comments. Others believe that a program should be completely self-documenting and that the Identification Division and internal comments should therefore describe the program completely. We take no stand on this issue.

As for the second variety of comments, we believe that good mnemonic words and carefully constructed code make the need for them minimal. For example, one should avoid comments that imitate the code, as in the following:

```
*          ** WE ARE DONE READING FROM SALESPERSON-
*          ** SALE-FILE AND WRITING INTO PAYROLL-FILE
   CLOSE   SALESPERSON-SALE-FILE,  PAYROLL-FILE.
```

Only when all else fails, and there is truly unusual code or an issue not clearly expressible in code, should one use English comment lines.

For an example of a good use of comments, refer back to Example 2.6b in the previous Proverb. Our final advice: Use comments effectively, but sparingly.

Proverb 12   USE MNEMONIC WORDS

It is difficult to overestimate the value of using good, mnemonic, user-defined words. It is all too easy to become careless and use words that later may complicate or confuse the intent of a program. Principles for selecting good mnemonic words are discussed at length in Chapter 5. Here it is sufficient to make one point: Use words that correctly reflect the objects they are intended to represent.

It is by no means an easy task to create the "best" menmonic word, but it is fairly easy to take a step in the right direction. Consider Example 2.7.

Example 2.7   Use of Good Mnemonic Words

```
EXAMPLE 2.7A   POOR

(1)     IF (TEMP = 98.6)
            PERFORM   TASK-0.


(2)     IF (S-SEM)
            PERFORM   PRODUCE-S-SEM-RPT.


(3)     COMPUTE   COST-ALL   ROUNDED = IM-QIS * IM-COST.

EXAMPLE 2.7B   BETTER


(1)     IF (TEMPERATURE = 98.6)
            PERFORM   RELEASE-PAT.


(2)     IF (SUM-SEMESTER)
            PERFORM   PRODUCE-SUM-SEMESTER-RPT.


(3)     COMPUTE   STOCK-COST   ROUNDED  =
                        QTY-IN-STOCK IN INPUT-MASTER-REC  *
                        ITEM-COST IN INPUT-MASTER-REC.

EXAMPLE 2.7C   BEST


(1)     IF (PATIENT-TEMPERATURE = 98.6)
            PERFORM   RELEASE-PATIENT.


(2)     IF (SUMMER-SEMESTER)
            PERFORM   PRODUCE-SUMMER-SEMESTER-RPT.


(3)     COMPUTE   ITEM-STOCK-VALUE   ROUNDED  =
                        QTY-IN-STOCK IN INVENTORY-ITEM-REC  *
                        UNIT-COST IN INVENTORY-ITEM-REC.
```

Whoever comes across sentences like those in Example 2.7a will be forced to scan program documentation, the Data Division, or other parts of the Procedure Division in order to pin down what words like TASK-0 and PRODUCE-S-SEM-RPT represent. The user-defined words in Example 2.7b are somewhat better. Once a maintenance programmer has acquainted himself with the program or looked back once or twice for the meanings of RELEASE-PAT and INPUT-MASTER-REC, he can get on with the needed modifications. Example 2.7c illustrates user-defined words that "speak for themselves." For the majority of readers, the words correctly reflect what they represent. More important, they do that the first time and every time.

In short, the major reason for using good, mnemonic, user-defined words is to improve readability. It is worth the initial extra time to devise and use informative words. A programmer may not fully appreciate the cost of using poor user-defined words until he has to debug or maintain a large program. The mnemonic assistance is then priceless.

Proverb 13   GET THE SYNTAX CORRECT NOW

How many times have you heard the COBOL language being roundly cursed for its highly sensitive syntax, or a COBOL compiler being criticized for not helping to add "trivial" missing spaces or periods? Consider the program fragments of Example 2.8a, which contain such trivial syntactic errors. These program fragments assume suitable data division entries. Example 2.8b shows the corresponding corrected versions. (Note: In implementations that relax some of the requirements of ANS COBOL, some of the constructs in Example 2.8a may be legal.) Errors like the ones in the first example should have been screened out in advance by a careful programmer. It is our contention that no errors, no matter how trivial, should pass the attention of a good programmer, for it is possible that some of them may not be detected by the compiler and will appear only after a program is in full operation.

Furthermore, there is little excuse for syntactic errors in programs, since the manual specifies the syntax for you. The time to consider syntax is not while verifying the completed program but while preparing it. Keep the manual or composite language skeleton handy as you write the code, and if you are not absolutely positive that the syntax of the statement you are writing is perfect, look it up. It only takes a few seconds, and your grasp of the language will increase with constant references to the manual. This work habit is all the more crucial if you are just learning COBOL or if you have done considerable programming in another language with similar but nevertheless different syntactic constructs.

You can and should write programs that are completely free of syntactic errors on the first run. We mean it. But to do so, you first must convince yourself that indeed you can do it. Second, you must get someone else to read

Example 2.8a   Incorrect Syntax

```
(1)      *********************************
         *                               *
         *        FOR EYES ONLY          *
         *                               *
         *********************************
         IDENTIFICATION DIVISION.


(2)          02 MARKER    PIC X(1), VALUE 1.


(3)          01 CRAFT-ID-INFO
                02 CRAFT-ID-DIGIT      PIC 9,    OCCURS 6 TIMES.
                02 CRAFT-ID-NUM        PIC 9(6), REDEFINES CRAFT-ID-DIGIT.


(4)          MOVE - 1 TO ADJUSTMENT.


(5)          MOVE BLANK TO  ERROR-INDICATOR.


(6)          MOVE 1 TO  TABLE-INDEX.


(7)          IF (CONDITION-A)
               PERFORM  PARA-A
             ELSE
               IF (CONDITION-B)
                 PERFORM  PARA-B
             PERFORM   PARA-X.


(8)          COMPUTE  B-FACTOR  ROUNDED = (ATTENDANCE)**0.5
                ON SIZE ERROR   MOVE 1 TO  COMPUTE-B-FACTOR-CONDITION.


(9)          INSPECT  CUSTOMER-ID-NUM
                REPLACING LEADING SPACES WITH ZEROS.


(10)         PERFORM  LIST-LIKELY-ERRORS IN ERROR-ANALYSIS SECTION.


(11)         MOVE 0 TO  DISTRICT (CURRENT-DISTRICT-SUBSCRIPT -1).


(12)         IF (X EQUALS Y)
               MOVE "*" TO INPUT-ERROR(6)
             ELSE
               NEXT SENTENCE.
```

Example 2.8b   Corrected Versions of Example 2.8a

```
(1)      IDENTIFICATION DIVISION.

         *********************************
         *                               *
         *        FOR EYES ONLY          *
         *                               *
         *********************************
```

Example 2.8b (cont'd)

```
(2)        02 MARKER   PIC X(1),  VALUE "1".


(3)     01 CRAFT-ID-INFO.
        02 CRAFT-ID-NUM        PIC 9(6).
        02 CRAFT-ID-DIGIT      REDEFINES  CRAFT-ID-NUMBER,
                               OCCURS 6 TIMES,  PIC 9.


(4)        MOVE -1 TO ADJUSTMENT.


(5)        MOVE SPACE TO  ERROR-INDICATOR.


(6)        SET  TABLE-INDEX  TO 1.


(7)        IF (CONDITION-A)
             PERFORM  PARA-A
           ELSE
             IF (CONDITION-B)
               PERFORM  PARA-B.
           PERFORM  PARA-X.


(8)        COMPUTE  B-FACTOR  ROUNDED = (ATTENDANCE) ** 0.5
             ON SIZE ERROR   MOVE 1 TO  COMPUTE-B-FACTOR-CONDITION.


(9)        INSPECT  CUSTOMER-ID-NUM
             REPLACING LEADING SPACES BY ZEROS.


(10)       PERFORM  LIST-LIKELY-ERRORS IN ERROR-ANALYSIS.


(11)       MOVE 0 TO  DISTRICT (CURRENT-DISTRICT-INDEX - 1).


(12)       IF (X  EQUAL  Y)
             MOVE "*" TO INPUT-ERROR(6)
           ELSE
             NEXT SENTENCE.
```

the work you produce (see Proverb 17). Just think of all the hours of turn-
around time you can waste tracking down simple syntactic errors, not to
mention some severe run-time problems that can be caused by them.

Proverb 14   PLAN FOR CHANGE

The result of this proverb is most valuable after a program is written—in
other words, during testing or program maintenance. The essential idea is to
make sure that all constant data items are recognized and given a value in the
Data Division. Furthermore, no statement in the Procedure Division should
modify these constant data items.

Example 2.9 Isolating Constants to Promote Easier Modification.

```
EXAMPLE 2.9A   POOR


        01 SALES-TABLE.
           02 DIVISION-SALES    OCCURS 6 TIMES
                                INDEXED BY DIVISION-INDEX,
                                PIC  9(6)V9(2),  COMP,  SYNC.
           ...


           PERFORM  ANALYZE-DIVISION-SALES
              VARYING  DIVISION-INDEX  FROM 1 BY 1
              UNTIL  (DIVISION-INDEX > 6).
           ...

           COMPUTE  AVG-SALES  ROUNDED  =  COMPANY-SALES / 6.




EXAMPLE 2.9B   BETTER


        02  NUM-OF-DIVISIONS     PIC 9(2),  COMP, SYNC, VALUE 6.
        ...

        01 SALES-TABLE.
           02 DIVISION-SALES    OCCURS 1 TO 12 TIMES
                                DEPENDING ON  NUM-OF-DIVISIONS
                                INDEXED BY  DIVISION-INDEX,
                                PIC  9(6)V9(2),  COMP,  SYNC.
           ...


           PERFORM  ANALYZE-DIVISION-SALES
              VARYING  DIVISION-INDEX  FROM 1 BY 1
              UNTIL  (DIVISION-INDEX > NUM-OF-DIVISIONS).
           ...

           COMPUTE  AVG-SALES  ROUNDED  =  COMPANY-SALES /
                                            NUM-OF-DIVISIONS.
```

Consider the programming situation of Example 2.9a. The programmer assumed that the company would always be organized into six divisions. The integer 6, besides its use in constructing Data Division tables, was used freely throughout the Procedure Division in computing averages and controlling conditions. When a company reorganization created eight divisions, changing the number of divisions to eight was a searching chore, for it was all too easy to neglect an occurrence of the integer 6. This is not the case with Example 2.9b, where a data name was created and given a value in the Data Division.

Nonnumeric literals also should be considered as constant data items. In Example 2.10a, we see the all too familiar situation of nonnumeric literals being plugged into ERROR-MESSAGE in various places throughout the program. There is a programming law stating roughly that every user will be dissatisfied with at least one of the program messages and will want to improve it. A corollary is that one of the better ways to tailor a software product to a user is

Example 2.10   Isolating Program Messages in the Data Division

```
EXAMPLE 2.10A   POOR

        MOVE "CONTROL CARD MISSING FROM FRONT OF INPUT CARD DECK."
                TO ERROR-MESSAGE.
        GENERATE ERROR-LINE.
        ...

        MOVE "ARE YOU SURE YOU HAVE THE RIGHT PROGRAM?"
                TO ERROR-MESSAGE.
        GENERATE ERROR-LINE.
        ...


EXAMPLE 2.10B   BETTER

    01 ERROR-TABLE.
       02 PROGRAM-USAGE-ERROR    PIC X(100),   VALUE
            "ARE YOU SURE YOU HAVE THE RIGHT PROGRAM?".
       02 CONTROL-CARD-ERROR     PIC X(100),   VALUE
            "CONTROL CARD MISSING FROM FRONT OF INPUT CARD DECK.".
        ...


        MOVE  CONTROL-CARD-ERROR  TO  ERROR-MESSAGE.
        GENERATE ERROR-LINE.
        ...

        MOVE  PROGRAM-USAGE-ERROR  TO  ERROR-MESSAGE.
        GENERATE ERROR-LINE.
```

to make it easy to change program messages. Example 2.10b gives a user that flexibility.

A second issue involved in planning for change concerns the so-called "magic numbers" such as those in Example 2.11a. How many times while reading a coded procedure have you been stumped by wondering what 0.03 and 0.01 are all about? A preceding comment line might help, but isn't the alternative of Example 2.11b much better?

The moral is simple: A well-designed program isolates constant data items in the Data Division. Program modification is made easier, and the reading of the Procedure Division is made less of a mystery. One will then need a larger and better organized Data Division, but this is a small, one-time price to pay for the benefits received.

Example 2.11   Handling Magic Numbers

```
EXAMPLE 2.11A   POOR

        COMPUTE CONTRIBUTIONS ROUNDED = (GROSS-PAY * 0.03) +
                                        (GROSS-PAY * 0.01).

EXAMPLE 2.11B   BETTER

        COMPUTE CONTRIBUTIONS ROUNDED = (GROSS-PAY * CARE-RATE) +
                                        (GROSS-PAY * POLITICAL-FUND-RATE).
```

Proverb 15 DON'T LEAVE THE READER IN THE DUST

Every programmer has a secret desire to produce a truly clever program. Shortening the code, running the program faster, or using fewer words are all popular pastimes. Resist this temptation, because the benefits seldom match the hidden costs. A good programmer writes code that is simple to read and quick to the point.

One way a programmer can keep code simple and clear is by avoiding COBOL constructs that, even after having been read previously, still make the reader stop and puzzle. Consider the code fragment,

IF (NOT POST-LENGTH > MIN-COL-LENGTH OR MAX-COL-LENGTH)

This forces the reader to consider carefully the COBOL condition evaluation rules. Consider also the fragment of Example 2.12a, which uses a nonstandard or implementation dependent feature of COBOL. In this case we not only lose

Example 2.12 Avoiding Nonstandard COBOL Features

```
EXAMPLE 2.12A   POOR


        01 SHIPMENT-TRANSACTION.
           02 NUM-SHIPPED        PIC 9(2).
              88 ILLEGAL-SHIPMENT        VALUES " ", " 1".
              88 QUESTIONABLE-SHIPMENT  VALUES 26 THROUGH 99.
           ...


           IF (ILLEGAL-SHIPMENT)
           ...
           ELSE
              IF (QUESTIONABLE-SHIPMENT)
              ...
              ELSE
              ...
                 SUBTRACT NUM-SHIPPED FROM QTY-IN-STOCK.


     EXAMPLE 2.12B   BETTER

        01 SHIPMENT-TRANSACTION.
           02 NUM-SHIPPED        PIC 9(2).
              88 ILLEGAL-SHIPMENT        VALUES 0, 1.
              88 QUESTIONABLE-SHIPMENT  VALUES 26 THROUGH 99.
           ...


           INSPECT NUM-SHIPPED
              REPLACING LEADING SPACES BY ZEROS.
           ...
           IF (ILLEGAL-SHIPMENT)
           ...
           ELSE
              IF (QUESTIONABLE-SHIPMENT)
              ...
              ELSE
              ...
                 SUBTRACT NUM-SHIPPED FROM QTY-IN-STOCK.
```

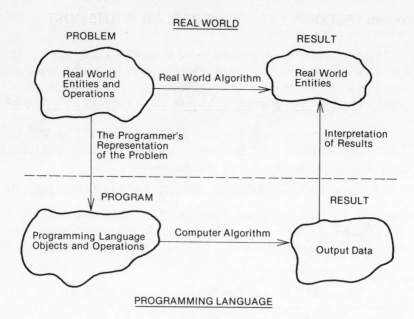

Fig. 2.5   Model for the programming task

clarity, but jeopardize program portability. This situation is rectified in Example 2.12b. We are not saying that one should avoid advanced COBOL features in general, for there are many advanced features that can be put to good use and that greatly clarify and simplify programs (see Proverb 18).

Generally, to avoid surprises for the reader, a programmer must be conscious that part of his job is to map real world entities (for example, payroll transactions, dollars, dates, and people's names) into the constructs of the COBOL language (for example, numbers and nonnumeric literals). A programmer must not only choose a particular representation for an entity, but must make sure that an operation validly represented in COBOL has meaning when applied to the original entity. For example, you can perform all arithmetic operations on numeric data. But while you can subtract two dollar amounts to get another dollar amount, it does not make sense to multiply two dollar amounts or take the square root of a dollar amount.

Consider Figure 2.5. The input to any program represents some class of real world entities: warehouse descriptions, part numbers, work cards, work hours, and the like. A computation is required to transform such entities into other entities, for example, an inventory, a new part number, a transaction file, or a salary. It is necessary to transform a computation manipulating these real world entities and operations into a program manipulating computer entities and operations. We shall say that a program is "natural" or "not tricky" if each step in the computer algorithm has a simple correspondence to a step in a real-world algorithm that a person would use to solve the problem. In other words, if the computer algorithm is analogous to the real-world algorithm, the program is "natural."

Naturalness is closely connected to the clarity and readability of programs. Often programs do not accurately reflect the real world algorithm that corresponds to a program's numeric, table, or string operations. The programmer soon learns that one of the hardest chores of programming is understanding the code written by another. For example, consider the following problem. You are given a list of 1,000 aircraft scheduling entries, each containing an aircraft ID number, port of availability, and time of availability. The entries are ordered by ascending aircraft ID number. In the scheduling of aircraft you must search and update this list many times, using a supposedly legal aircraft ID number. Example 2.13 illustrates two pieces of code to do the job. Try to understand why each one does just that before continuing.

Example 2.13a was written to make the searching process fast. Example 2.13b was written to solve the problem with a straightforward approach. While the first program is probably faster, it leaves many readers in the dust. In fact

Example 2.13a Emphasizing Speed Over Clarity

```
*                ** THE AIRCRAFT AVAILABILITY INFORMATION IS STORED
*                **    IN ROW-MAJOR ORDER BY ASCENDING VALUE
*                **    OF AIRCRAFT ID NUM.

    01 AIRCRAFT-AVAILABILITY-TABLE.
       02  X        OCCURS 10 TIMES  INDEXED BY X-INDEX.
          03  Y        OCCURS 10 TIMES  INDEXED BY Y-INDEX.
             04  Z        OCCURS 10 TIMES  INDEXED BY Z-INDEX.
                05 AIRCRAFT-ID-NUM        PIC 9(6).
                05 PORT-OF-AVAILABILITY   PIC X(4).
                05 TIME-OF-AVAILABILITY   PIC 9(4).
       ...


    PERFORM  FIND-DESIRED-CRAFT-AVAILABILITY.
    MOVE  Z (X-INDEX, Y-INDEX, Z-INDEX)
          TO  DESIRED-CRAFT-AVAILABILITY.
       ...

    FIND-DESIRED-CRAFT-AVAILABILITY.
       SET  X-INDEX, Y-INDEX, Z-INDEX  TO 1.
       SEARCH  X
          AT END    SET  X-INDEX TO 10
          WHEN  (AIRCRAFT-ID-NUM (X-INDEX, Y-INDEX, Z-INDEX)
                   > DESIRED-CRAFT-ID-NUM )
             SET  X-INDEX  DOWN BY 1.

       SEARCH  Y
          AT END    SET  Y-INDEX TO 10
          WHEN  (AIRCRAFT-ID-NUM (X-INDEX, Y-INDEX, Z-INDEX)
                   > DESIRED-CRAFT-ID-NUM )
             SET  Y-INDEX  DOWN BY 1.

       SEARCH  Z
          WHEN  (AIRCRAFT-ID-NUM (X-INDEX, Y-INDEX, Z-INDEX)
                   = DESIRED-CRAFT-ID-NUM )
             NEXT SENTENCE.
```

Example 2.13b   Emphasizing Clarity Over Speed

```
*            ** THE AIRCRAFT AVAILABILITY INFORMATION IS STORED
*            **   IN ORDER BY ASCENDING VALUE OF
*            **   AIRCRAFT ID NUM.
   01 AIRCRAFT-AVAILABILITY-TABLE.
      02 AIRCRAFT-AVAILABILITY     OCCURS 1000 TIMES
                                   INDEXED BY AVAILABILITY-INDEX.
         03 AIRCRAFT-ID-NUM        PIC 9(5).
         03 PORT-OF-AVAILABILITY   PIC X(7).
         03 TIME-OF-AVAILABILITY   PIC 9(4).
   ...


   SET AVAILABILITY-INDEX TO 1.
   SEARCH AIRCRAFT-AVAILABILITY
      WHEN  ( AIRCRAFT-ID-NUM (AVAILABILITY-INDEX)  =
                                 DESIRED-CRAFT-ID-NUM )
         NEXT SENTENCE.

   MOVE  AIRCRAFT-AVAILABILITY (AVAILABILITY-INDEX)
         TO DESIRED-CRAFT-AVAILABILITY.
```

the person who generated the first program missed a lucid alternative solution similar to that of Example 2.13b. Do you know what it is?

Another area where natural programs have an advantage is that of extendability. Because a natural algorithm is analogous to real-world operations, extensions can often be made easily. Since a tricky algorithm usually depends on specific properties of numbers, nonnumeric literals, or elaborate data structures, it usually cannot be applied easily or at all to cases other than the original problem. Example 2.13 illustrates this point well. Try to extend the programs to search for the correct availability information when there are 1,500 aircraft to consider.

Before concluding the discussion of this proverb, remember that when tricks are indiscriminately employed, good structure, flexibility, and clarity are frequently lost. Merging two or more modules of code in order to wring out those "extra lines" or adding a few lines in order to gain efficiency are both easy ways to prevent anyone from following the program. Not to mention the extra time needed to develop the special wrinkle and the extra testing time needed to check the new and often subtle boundary conditions, are you sure that fewer machine instructions or faster machine execution is likely?

One last point about tricky or clever programming must be mentioned. There are cases where tricky methods are in fact justified, for example, to provide demanded efficiency of execution or economy of storage. However, before you resort to tricky programming, you should have a clear reason for doing so. Moreover, you should estimate the actual gain such programming will yield. Otherwise, you should stick to operations and objects that have a natural analog in the real world.

Proverb 16   PREPARE TO PROVE THE PUDDING

We have advocated the top-down approach to program development. In turn, we now advocate the top-down approach to checking program correctness, which consists of verifying the main program and the upper levels first and the most primitive modules last.

Verifying from the top down should seem obvious, especially if a program is being written top-down. Programs of this type are usually well modularized, and it is unwise to verify lower levels if the upper levels may be incorrect. Since the sections of the program are integral units that can stand on their own, the most important ones should be verified first. A schematic illustration of a program is presented in Fig. 2.6. Encircled sections indicate that the set of enclosed modules is to be considered as a unit. The program has five main modules, each of which can be verified separately. Some of these modules call

THE PROGRAM P

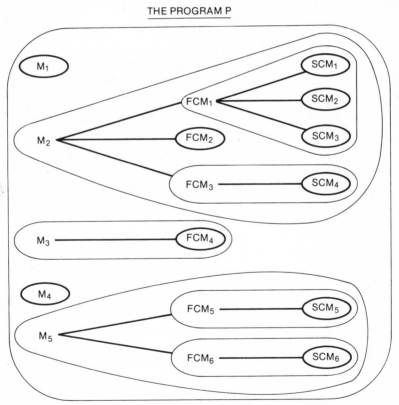

P - The Entire Program   FCM - First Called Submodules
M - Main Modules   SCM - Second Called Submodules

Fig. 2.6   Picture of a program designed top down

submodules, which in turn call other more deeply nested modules. The verification process starts with the main program As upper modules are verified, the process continues through levels until the entire program has been verified. Verifying the complete program in one lump sum is to be avoided.

What are some of the available COBOL verification aids? Foremost, try to write programs that run correctly the first time. Adhere to good COBOL programming principles. The better the quality of the program to begin with (good design, development, and documentation), the less likely it is that a serious error might occur, and the more likely it is that you will find those that do occur. Second, judiciously use the COBOL debug module to create an external record of the operation of the program.

A wise usage of the COBOL debugging module has several aspects. Most important, strategic locations for verification aids will suggest themselves while you are writing the program. For example, one can dump selective information in a crucial procedure or subprogram, or trace the values of an active variable or volatile file. If you initially take time during writing the program to insert verification aids, you will save time in the long run. Otherwise, if there is an aborted run (optimists get only unpleasant surprises), it will take much longer and be less fruitful if you have to go back over the program to find the best places for verification aids. When the program is running correctly, it will take only a few seconds to remove the verification portions, if they need to be

Example 2.14a   Using Debugging Lines

```
D          PERFORM  DUMP-BEFORE-GET-FUTURE-DATE.
        CALL "GET-FUTURE-DATE"
          USING  BASE-DATE,  NUM-DAYS-HENCE,  FUTURE-DATE.

D          PERFORM  DUMP-AFTER-GET-FUTURE-DATE.
        MOVE  FUTURE-DATE  TO  NEXT-INDUCTION-DATE.
        ...

D VERIFICATION-I-O  SECTION.
D
D DUMP-AFTER-GET-FUTURE-DATE.
D    DISPLAY "AFTER SUBPROGRAM   GET-FUTURE-DATE :"
D       UPON VERIFICATION-PRINTER.
D
D    DISPLAY "     BASE-DATE = ",  BASE-DATE,
D           "     NUM-DAYS-HENCE = ",  NUM-DAYS-HENCE,
D           "     FUTURE-DATE = ",  FUTURE-DATE
D       UPON VERIFICATION-PRINTER.
D
D
D DUMP-BEFORE-GET-FUTURE-DATE.
D    DISPLAY SPACES  UPON VERIFICATION-PRINTER.
D    DISPLAY "BEFORE SUBPROGRAM   GET-FUTURE-DATE :"
D       UPON VERIFICATION-PRINTER.
D
D    DISPLAY "     BASE-DATE = ",  BASE-DATE,
D           "     NUM-DAYS-HENCE = ",  NUM-DAYS-HENCE,
D           "     FUTURE-DATE = ",  FUTURE-DATE
D       UPON VERIFICATION-PRINTER.
```

Example 2.14b Employing the USE FOR DEBUGGING Statement

```
PROCEDURE DIVISION.


DECLARATIVES.

VERIFY-COUNTY-UNEMPLOYMENT  SECTION.
    USE FOR DEBUGGING ON  ANALYZE-COUNTY-UNEMPLOYMENT.

   DUMP-HDR-AND-SNAPSHOT.
    IF (COUNTY-SUBSCRIPT = 1)
        DISPLAY SPACES  UPON VERIFICATION-PRINTER
        DISPLAY "BEFORE FIRST USE OF ANALYZE-COUNTY-UNEMPLOYMENT:"
        UPON VERIFICATION-PRINTER
    ELSE
        DISPLAY "BEFORE NEXT:" UPON VERIFICATION-PRINTER.

    DISPLAY "    COUNTY-SUBSCRIPT = ", COUNTY-SUBSCRIPT,
            "    NUM-UNEMPLOYED-IN-STATE = ",
                            NUM-UNEMPLOYED-IN-STATE,
            "    COUNTY-MOST-UNEMPLOYED = ",
                            COUNTY-MOST-UNEMPLOYED,
            "    COUNTY-HIGHEST-UNEMPLOY-RATE = ",
                            COUNTY-HIGHEST-UNEMPLOY-RATE
        UPON VERIFICATION-PRINTER.

END DECLARATIVES.

    ...

    PERFORM  ANALYZE-COUNTY-UNEMPLOYMENT
        VARYING  COUNTY-SUBSCRIPT  FROM 1 BY 1
        UNTIL (COUNTY-SUBSCRIPT > NUM-COUNTIES-IN-STATE).
```

---

removed. For all this, be moderate in your use of verificiation aids. It is best, especially in verification runs of rather large sections of code, to use aids which merely try to isolate an oversight to one area of code. Example 2.14a shows the use of debugging lines that compile when the DEBUGGING MODE clause is specified. Example 2.14b shows the use of the USE FOR DEBUGGING statement.

Systems which implement COBOL usually offer verification facilities beyond those which are found in the language. Does your system support any program design, development, or documentation aids? Does your system support a cross-reference lister, program librarian, test data generator, test supervisor, module testing, execution monitor, or output analyzer package? Be sure to find out what features your system provides, and incorporate them into programs you write. Although it may not be wise to use implementation-dependent features as part of a final program, it would be more than foolish not to utilize them for verification.

In summary, you can and should make good use of the verification facilities in COBOL and in your computer system. Remember, blessed is he who expects the worst, for he shall not be disappointed.

Proverb 17   HAVE SOMEONE ELSE READ THE WORK

A COBOL programmer must realize that programming is by no means a personal art. While poor definitions, documentation, and programs can be easy for him to overlook, they will be quite evident to someone else. Even good programmers stand to gain by having others read the work being produced. This proverb is so important that we considered putting it at the head of the list.

Example 2.15   The COBOL Compiler Catches One Error, But Who Catches the Other?

```
PROCEDURE DIVISION     USING   NUMBER,  DESIRED-MODULUS,
                               CHECK-DIGIT-CHAR, RESULT-CONDITION.

    MAIN-PROGRAM.
      PERFORM CHECK-INPUT-ARGUMENTS.
      IF (INPUT-ARGUMENTS-ERROR)
        MOVE  INPUT-ARGUMENTS-CONDITION  TO  RESULT-CONDITION
        MOVE  ERROR-CHECK-DIGIT-CHAR  TO  CHECK-DIGIT-CHAR
      ELSE
        PERFORM  CALC-CHECK-DIGIT-NUM.
        IF (CALC-CHECK-DIGIT-ERROR)
          MOVE  CHECK-DIGIT-CALC-CONDITION  TO  RESULT-CONDITION
          MOVE  ERROR-CHECK-DIGIT-CHAR  TO  CHECK-DIGIT-CHAR
        ELSE
          MOVE ZERO TO  RESULT-CONDITION
          MOVE ALPHABETIC-CHAR(CHECK-DIGIT-NUM)
               TO CHECK-DIGIT-CHAR.

    RETURN-TO-CALLER.
      EXIT PROGRAM.


    CHECK-INPUT-ARGUMENTS.
      IF (NUMBER NOT NUMERIC)
        MOVE 1 TO  INPUT-ARGUMENTS-CONDITION
      ELSE
        IF (DESIRED-MODULUS  NOT NUMERIC)
           OR (NOT  LEGAL-DESIRED-MODULUS)
          MOVE 2 TO  INPUT-ARGUMENTS-CONDITION
        ELSE
          MOVE ZERO TO  INPUT-ARGUMENTS-CONDITION.

    CALC-CHECK-DIGIT-NUM.
      MOVE ZERO TO  WEIGHTED-SUM.
      MOVE ZERO TO  WEIGHTED-SUM-CALC-CONDITION.
      PERFORM CALC-WEIGHTED-SUM
        VARYING I FROM 1 BY 1
        UNTIL ( (I > MAX-LENGTH-COBOL-INTEGER) OR
                            WEIGHTED-SUM-CALC-ERROR).
      IF (WEIGHTED-SUM-CALC-ERROR)
        MOVE 3 TO  CHECK-DIGIT-CALC-CONDITION
      ELSE
        MOVE ZERO TO  CHECK-DIGIT-CALC-CONDITION
        DIVIDE  WEIGHTED-SUM  BY  DESIRED-MODULUS
          GIVING  INTEGER-QUOTIENT
          REMAINDER  INTEGER-REMAINDER
        COMPUTE  CHECK-DIGIT-NUM  =  DESIRED-MODULUS -
                                     INTEGER-REMAINDER.

    CALC-WEIGHTED-SUM.
      COMPUTE  WEIGHTED-SUM  =  WEIGHTED-SUM +
                          (NUMBER-DIGIT (I) * DIGIT-WEIGHT (I))
          ON SIZE ERROR   MOVE 1 TO  WEIGHTED-SUM-CALC-CONDITION.
```

Having someone else read the work does not mean just having someone else read the final code. Even a developing problem definition ought to be read by someone else. The program specifications, the levels of the top-down design, and the test plans you are writing also should be read. All of these projects should be double checked by someone else's eyes.

The primary benefit of this second reading is that it helps weed out quickly all unwarranted assumptions, unintentional omissions, unnecessary complexities, or just plain mistakes. However, there are other benefits. Both you and your reader can learn good problem solving and programming techniques from one another. Programming teams that make a point of work-reading foster cooperative communication, maintain team standards more easily, promote quality documentation, and consistently keep abreast of the total work effort.

Consider Example 2.15, which contains two simple but easily made errors. The programmer who wrote the code would find the errors almost impossible to detect by rereading the code yet another time. Try to find them yourself. We contend that work-reading will help prevent such errors from ever disturbing your sleep.

We have a few suggestions for making work-reading more effective. First, remember the proverbs, and point out any violations you see. Second, choose a sample input; then calculate the output as if you were the computer. Assume nothing and use exactly what is written. See that each module performs correctly. If the program is too long or complex to check in its entirety, then check each major section first, and later check the smaller units, assuming that the major sections are correct. Third, take special care to watch for the boundary conditions and other special cases. Failure to account for these is one of the most critical programming errors.

The time and extra care required for work-reading seem a small price to pay for all the benefits listed above. However, at first the practice may seem time consuming, annoying, and even possibly embarrassing. You must make an extra effort to stick by this proverb for quite a while. Given time, it will come to have an enormous beneficial impact on your work. As a helpful hint we recommend that you practice as a reader for others. Remember, *all aspects of good programming practice are fostered by work-reading.*

Proverb 18 READ THE MANUAL AGAIN

Now why would anyone want to go back and read those boring language or system manuals again? A wise programmer will occasionally do exactly that. After programming for a while, one tends to restrict oneself to a convenient subset of the COBOL language or the host computer system. As a result many useful features may be neglected. Periodically rereading the manuals will help to keep useful features in mind when the need for them arises.

Example 2.16   Use of the LINAGE Clause and the END-OF-PAGE Phrase

```
FD REPORT-FILE
    RECORD CONTAINS 120 CHARACTERS,
    LABEL RECORDS OMITTED,
    LINAGE IS 60 LINES, LINES AT TOP 3, LINES AT BOTTOM 3.
01 RPT-LINE     PIC X(120).
...

    MOVE 1 TO  CURRENT-PAGE-NUM.
...

PRODUCE-CARD-IMAGE-LINE.
    IF (LINAGE-COUNTER = 1)
        MOVE  CURRENT-PAGE-NUM  TO  PAGE-NUM IN PAGE-HEADER
        MOVE  PAGE-HEADER  TO  RPT-LINE
        PERFORM  FREE-RPT-LINE
        PERFORM  PRODUCE-LINE-SKIP  3 TIMES.
    MOVE  NEW-SEQUENCE-NUM IN OUTPUT-DATA-ITEMS
          TO  SEQUENCE-NUM-AREA IN CARD-IMAGE-LINE.
    MOVE  INDICATOR-A-B-AREAS IN OLD-SOURCE-CARD
          TO  INDICATOR-A-B-AREAS IN CARD-IMAGE-LINE.
    MOVE  NEW-PROGRAM-ID IN OUTPUT-DATA-ITEMS
          TO  PROGRAM-ID-AREA IN CARD-IMAGE-LINE.
    MOVE  CARD-IMAGE-LINE  TO  RPT-LINE.
    PERFORM  FREE-RPT-LINE.
...

PRODUCE-LINE-SKIP.
    MOVE SPACES TO  RPT-LINE.
    PERFORM  FREE-RPT-LINE.

FREE-RPT-LINE.
    WRITE  RPT-LINE
       BEFORE ADVANCING 1 LINE
       AT END-OF-PAGE    ADD 1 TO  CURRENT-PAGE-NUM.
```

One particular area of COBOL in which there is much to forget involves input and output. The Report Writer makes it possible to create complex reports without expending much effort on allocation of spaces, counters, and formatting. While it does take quite a bit of reading and practice to feel at ease with the Report Writer, it is fairly easy to use. Another, less elaborate aid to report writing, is the LINAGE clause and the END-OF-PAGE phrase. Example 2.16 illustrates the use of this simpler but still effective feature.

Consider also the following situation. Suppose that you were asked to append to a sequential MASTER file a similarly sorted sequential APPEND-TO-MASTER file. You could write a 30 to 40 line procedure that copies the MASTER file to a COPY-OF-MASTER file, then copies COPY-OF-MASTER back over the original MASTER, and immediately copies APPEND-TO-MASTER on the end of this new MASTER. Even better, you could write a shorter procedure that uses an OPEN statement with the EXTEND phrase to position the MASTER file for writing immediately following the last logical record. Also you could use the MERGE statement directly.

One of the common complaints with COBOL programs has to do with program length. As a result, there is an incentive to write short, and usually uninformative, user-defined words. The COBOL COPY statement is a feature which can be used to help minimize this problem. Let's suppose that it takes you and others 50 to 60 lines to code the FD and O1 entries for a commonly used inventory file. By putting this text in a library, everyone can reference the same code merely by writing

COPY INVENTORY-FILE-FD-016.

The compiler will insert the correct text into the source program. This practice not only saves coding effort, but helps prevent coding errors.

It is common to build verification aids into a program as you are coding. Typically, one uses the DISPLAY statement with the UPON phrase. However, when verification is completed (ha!), it is a chore to remove these statements from the source program. Moreover, once they are removed, it is almost certain that a oversight will appear which will require their reinsertion. A COBOL feature of great help here is the ability to code these DISPLAY statements as debugging lines with "D ' in the indicator area. These permanent debugging lines can be optionally compiled or treated as comments, depending on the respective presence or absence of the DEBUGGING MODE clause in the SOURCE-COMPUTER paragraph in the Environment Division.

We have mentioned just a few of the many useful but often underused COBOL features. There are many others. Furthermore, the manual for your particular computer system is likely to describe many additional facilities for general programming use. System supported programming tools are notoriously underused.

One must be careful when using unfamiliar or little used features. Be sure you are using them correctly. Do not go overboard, for the results may no longer be simple and direct (see Proverb 15). Nevertheless, we strongly recommend an occasional look at the manuals. You may be pleased with what you find.

Proverb 19 DON'T BE AFRAID TO START OVER

This is the last proverb, but it is of great importance. We dare not dwell on it too long, because we hope you will never have to use it.

Sometimes during program development, testing, or modification, it may occur to a programmer that the program he is working with is becoming unusually cumbersome. So many user-requirement changes may have occurred that the problem is now different from what it was originally. Very few, if any, of the programming proverbs may have been applied in developing the program; or perhaps the program produces error after error.

Pruning and restoring a blighted tree is almost an imposssible task. The same is true of blighted computer programs. Restoring a structure that has been distorted by patches and deletions or fixing a program with a seriously weak algorithm just isn't worth the time. The best that can result is a long, inefficient, unintelligible program that defies further maintenance. The worst that could result we dare not think of. When you seem hopelessly in trouble, start over. Lessons painfully learned on the old program can be applied to the new one to yield the desired result in far less time with far less trouble.

This last proverb may seem heartless, but don't let your ego stand in the way. Don't be afraid to start over. We mean *really* start over. Don't fall into the trap of trying to convert a bad program into a good one.

EXERCISES

Exercise 2.1 (Define the Problem Completely)

With a good problem specification, any two programs written to solve the problem would have exactly the same input/output characteristics. Consider the following problem specification:

"Write a COBOL subprogram that assigns to an alphanumeric data item the current date in standard form (e.g., 75 SEP 08)."

Upon careful thought, the above specification reveals points that would be unclear to a programmer. Rewrite the specification to define the problem completely. (Note: You are to write a problem specification, not a program.)

Exercise 2.2 (Define the Problem Completely)

The following problem definition is unclear at a number of points. List ten things missing from the definition. Then assume you know what the user needs, and construct a complete definition of the problem. (Hint: You may want to read Irene's functional specification in Chapter 3.)

Problem specification: Statistics are recorded for every program compiled or run on the computer at the Programmer's Equity Life Insurance Company. A record has the following format:

Program Statistics Record

Bytes	Meaning
1–4	Account ID
5–35	Program ID
36–37	Compilation time (*minutes*)
38–40	Number of compilation errors
41–43	Allotted main memory (*in thousands of words*)
44–46	Execution time (*minutes*)
47	Execution aborted?
48–51	Cost

A report must be made for the first-line manager in charge of each account. The report must have statistics that summarize total compilation time, total compilation errors, maximum allotted main memory, total execution time, total abnormal terminations, and total costs for each program that was compiled or run during the week. The statistics should appear in alphabetical order by program ID. The end of the report should give the weekly total computer cost.

Exercise 2.3 (Start the Documentation Early)
Discuss the method by which a high-quality, multi-volume reference book set is written, its overall format, and how subjects are presented. What reference set features might be applied to the writing of program documentation?

Exercise 2.4 (Use PERFORM and CALL)
If you have use for the subprogram alluded to in Exercise 2.1, then write it. Moreover, use it!

Exercise 2.5 (Use PERFORM and CALL; Don't Be Afraid to Start Over)
Start from the top and redo the following program fragment, using the PERFORM and CALL features effectively.

```
PROCEDURE DIVISION.

PREPROCESS.
    OPEN INPUT    DECK.
    OPEN OUTPUT   DISK-FILE,
                  CARD-ERROR-DECK,
                  PROGRAM-ACTION-RPT.
    MOVE 0 TO   DECK-CONDITION,
                CARD-ERROR-DECK-CONDITION,
                SIZE-DISK-FILE.
    MOVE -1 TO  ID-NUM-CARD-LAST-COPIED.
```

```
PROCESS-NEXT-SALESPERSON-CARD.
   READ DECK
      AT END    GO TO  PRODUCE-PROGRAM-ACTION-RPT.

   MOVE SPACES TO  CARD-ERROR-LIST.
*               ** CHECK THE CONTENTS OF ALL FIELDS OF SALESPERSON-CARD
   INSPECT  ID-NUM IN SALESPERSON-CARD
   REPLACING LEADING SPACES BY ZEROS.
   IF (ID-NUM IN SALESPERSON-CARD  IS NOT NUMERIC)
      MOVE "*" TO  CARD-ERROR (1).
   IF (LAST-NAME IN SALESPERSON-CARD  IS NOT ALPHABETIC)
      MOVE "*" TO  CARD-ERROR (2).
   INSPECT  SALES-LAST-PERIOD IN SALESPERSON-CARD
   REPLACING LEADING SPACES BY ZEROS.
   IF (SALES-LAST-PERIOD IN SALESPERSON-CARD  IS NOT NUMERIC)
      MOVE "*" TO  CARD-ERROR (3).

*            ** CHECK THAT SALESPERSON-CARD IS IN ASCENDING
*            ** SEQUENCE BY ID-NUM
   IF (ID-NUM IN SALESPERSON-CARD  <  ID-NUM-CARD-LAST-COPIED)
      MOVE "*" TO  CARD-ERROR (4)
   ELSE
      IF (ID-NUM IN SALESPERSON-CARD  =  ID-NUM-CARD-LAST-COPIED)
         MOVE "*" TO  CARD-ERROR (5).

   IF (NOT LEGAL-SALESPERSON-CARD)
      MOVE 1 TO  CARD-ERROR-DECK-CONDITION
      MOVE SPACES TO  CARD-ERROR-REC
      MOVE CORRESPONDING  SALESPERSON-CARD  TO  CARD-ERROR-REC
      MOVE CARD-ERROR-LIST  TO  ERROR-CODINGS IN CARD-ERROR-REC
      WRITE CARD-ERROR-REC
   ELSE
      MOVE SALESPERSON-CARD  TO  DISK-REC
      WRITE DISK-REC
      ADD 1 TO  SIZE-DISK-FILE
      MOVE ID-NUM IN SALESPERSON-CARD  TO  ID-NUM-CARD-LAST-COPIED.
   GO TO  PROCESS-NEXT-SALESPERSON-CARD.



PRODUCE-PROGRAM-ACTION-RPT.
   PERFORM GET-ANSI-DATE.
   MOVE ANSI-TODAYS-DATE
         TO TODAYS-DATE IN PROGRAM-ACTION-RPT-HEADER.
   WRITE RPT-LINE FROM PROGRAM-ACTION-RPT-HEADER
      AFTER ADVANCING PAGE.

   IF (NOT EMPTY-CARD-ERROR-DECK)
      WRITE RPT-LINE FROM ERROR-DECK-NOT-EMPTY-MESSAGE
         AFTER ADVANCING 3 LINES.

   MOVE SIZE-DISK-FILE
         TO FILE-SIZE IN DISK-FILE-STATUS-MESSAGE.
   WRITE RPT-LINE FROM  DISK-FILE-STATUS-MESSAGE
      AFTER ADVANCING 3 LINES.

   MOVE SPACES TO  RPT-LINE.
   WRITE RPT-LINE
      BEFORE ADVANCING PAGE.


POSTPROCESS.
   CLOSE  DECK,
          DISK-FILE,
          CARD-ERROR-DECK,
          PROGRAM-ACTION-RPT.
   STOP RUN.

COPY PROC-GET-ANSI-DATE.
```

Exercise 2.6 (Don't GO TO)
Develop two more alternatives for Table 2.2 to avoid using a GO TO statement.

Exercise 2.7 (Don't GO TO)
If your COBOL implementation supports the PERFORM statement with the UNTIL phrase, then assume the next program you write will be graded by using the formula,

GRADE = 100 − (10 X (number of GO TOs in program))

or

GRADE = 0

whichever is greater.

Exercise 2.8 (Prettyprint)
Discuss the pros and cons of prettyprinting the IF statement as

IF <condition>
   <statement>
 ELSE
   <statement>

instead of

IF <condition>
  <statement>
ELSE
  <statement>

as was advised in the Appendix.

Exercise 2.9 (Prettyprint)
The following program was written at an installation that forbids the use of condition names. Prettyprint the program. (Hint: You first may want to read Chapter 4.)

```
IDENTIFICATION DIVISION.
PROGRAM-ID. CHECK-MONTH-ABBR.
*RELEASE 75-A
 INSTALLATION. COMPACT PROGRAM CORPORATION, COBOLIA.
*     FOR INPUT THIS PROGRAM EXPECTS A POSSIBLE MONTH
*ABBREVIATION THAT IS AN ALPHANUMERIC ITEM OCCUPYING THREE
*CHARACTER POSITIONS.
*     FOR OUTPUT THIS PROGRAM RETURNS A VALUE OF 0 OR 1 FOR A
*SINGLE DIGIT INTEGER ITEM.  A RETURNED VALUE OF 1 INDICATES
*THAT THE INPUT ABBREVIATION IS AN ANSI STANDARD MONTH
*ABBREVIATION; 0 INDICATES IT IS NOT.
 ENVIRONMENT DIVISION.
 CONFIGURATION SECTION.
 SOURCE-COMPUTER. TINY-1.
 OBJECT-COMPUTER. TINY-1.
 DATA DIVISION.
```

```
WORKING-STORAGE SECTION.
1    ANSI-MONTH-ABBR-TABLE.
2    MONTH-ABBR-LIST.
3      JANUARY-ABBR PIC X(3) VALUE "JAN".
3      FEBRUARY-ABBR PIC X(3) VALUE "FEB".
3      MARCH-ABBR PIC X(3) VALUE "MAR".
3      APRIL-ABBR PIC X(3) VALUE "APR".
3      MAY-ABBR PIC(3) VALUE "MAY".
3      JUNE-ABBR PIC X(3) VALUE "JUN".
3      JULY-ABBR PIC X(3) VALUE "JUL".
3      AUGUST-ABBR PIC X(3) VALUE "AUG".
3      SEPTEMBER-ABBR PIC X(3) VALUE "SEP".
3      OCTOBER-ABBR PIC X(3) VALUE "OCT".
3      NOVEMBER-ABBR PIC X(3) VALUE "NOV".
3      DECEMBER-ABBR PIC X(3) VALUE "DEC".
2    MONTH-ABBR REDEFINES MONTH-ABBR-LIST PIC X(3) OCCURS 12
       TIMES INDEXED BY MONTH-NUM-INDEX.
LINKAGE SECTION.
77   QUESTIONABLE-MONTH-ABBR PIC X(3).
77   OK-INDICATOR-NUM PIC 9.
PROCEDURE DIVISION USING QUESTIONABLE-MONTH-ABBR OK-INDICATOR-
-    NUM.
MAIN-PROGRAM. SET MONTH-NUM-INDEX TO 1.  SEARCH MONTH-ABBR
       AT END MOVE 0 TO OK-INDICATOR-NUM WHEN QUESTIONABLE-MONTH-ABB
-      R = MONTH-ABBR(MONTH-NUM-INDEX) MOVE 1 TO OK-INDICATOR-NUM.
RETURN-TO-CALLER. EXIT PROGRAM.
```

Exercise 2.10 (Comment Effectively)

Some programmers believe that a person reading the code, *not* the programmer, should insert in-line comment lines (see Proverb 11). Discuss and experiment with this practice. As a start you may want to insert in-line comments into Example 2.6b of Proverb 10.

Exercise 2.11 (Use Mnemonic Words)

The following code fragment performs a well-known arithmetic computation. By merely changing the user-defined words, rewrite the fragment so that the intended computation is clear.

```
02 TWO      PIC 9,  COMP,  VALUE 2.
02 FOUR     PIC 9,  COMP,  VALUE 4.
...
01 LEFT-MIDDLE-RIGHT.
   02 LEFT-SIDE      PIC   9(4)V9(4).
   02 MIDDLE         PIC   9(4)V9(4).
   02 RIGHT-SIDE     PIC   9(4)V9(4).
   02 FILLER         PIC   X(56).
...


MOVE ZERO TO  STAT.
...

PERFORM  NEW-LEFT-MIDDLE-RIGHT.
IF (STAT = ZERO)
   PERFORM  ONE-AND-OTHER
   IF (COMP-COND = ZERO)
      ...

ONE-AND-OTHER.
   IF (LEFT-SIDE  NOT EQUAL ZERO)
      COMPUTE  RIGHT-1  ROUNDED  =  FOUR * LEFT-SIDE * RIGHT-SIDE
      COMPUTE  TEMP  ROUNDED     =  (MIDDLE * MIDDLE) - RIGHT-1
      IF (TEMP  NOT LESS THAN ZERO)
         COMPUTE  RIGHT-2  ROUNDED  =  TEMP ** 0.5
```

```
        COMPUTE   ONE      ROUNDED . =  ( - MIDDLE + RIGHT-2) /
                                           (TWO * LEFT-SIDE)
        COMPUTE   OTHER    ROUNDED  =  ( - MIDDLE - RIGHT-2) /
                                           (TWO * LEFT-SIDE)
           MOVE 0 TO COMP-COND
        ELSE
           MOVE 2 TO COMP-COND
     ELSE
        MOVE 1 TO  COMP-COND.
     ...

  NEW-LEFT-MIDDLE-RIGHT.
     READ INNI INTO  LEFT-MIDDLE-RIGHT
        AT END   MOVE 1 TO STAT.
```

Exercise 2.12 (Get the Syntax Correct Now)

Which of the following examples are syntactically correct? Correct the erroneous examples. *You may assume any appropriate Data Division entry to make an example legal.*

```
(1)    FILE SECTION.

          FD DECK.
             ...
          01 SALE-REC.
             ...
          FD DISK-FILE.
             ...
          01 SALE-REC.


(2)       02 BIG-NUM            PIC  9(19).  VALUE +10000000000000000000.

(3)       02 INITIALS     PIC  A(6),  VALUE "L.J.C.".

(4)       OPEN INPUT    DECK,
               OUTPUT   RPT-FILE.

(5)       MOVE 21 TO  ALPHANUMERIC-ITEM.

(6)       MOVE 21. TO  ALPHANUMERIC-ITEM.

(7)        ** NUMERIC-ITEM IS DESCRIBED AS   9(3)V9
          MOVE "123.4" TO  NUMERIC-ITEM.

(8)       IF (123 = "123")
             ...

(9)       IF (4 IS NOT ZERO)
             ...

(10)      IF (NOT  EOF-DECK)
             ADD 10 TO  NEW-SEQUENCE-NUM IN OUTPUT-ITEMS
                ON SIZE ERROR   MOVE 1 TO  PROGRAM-STATUS
             IF (PROGRAM-ABORT)
                NEXT SENTENCE
             ELSE
                ...
          ELSE
             NEXT SENTENCE.

(11)      COMPUTE  ROOT-1  ROUNDED  =  (- B + SQRT-DISCRM) / (2 * A).
```

Exercise 2.13   (Plan for Change)

Consider the following two program fragments, which were written for an insurance program. Both do the required job. However, the second fragment loads the Data Division and unclutters the Procedure Division in anticipation of change (Proverb 14). Discuss whether such planning for change is too extreme. Be sure to consider the use of the COPY verb.

```
FRAGMENT 1


   01 INSURANCE-RATES-TABLE.
      02 AGE-GROUPS-RATES.
         03 AGE-1-20-RATE        PIC  V9(3),  VALUE 0.100.
         03 AGE-21-40-RATE       PIC  V9(3),  VALUE C.067.
         03 AGE-41-60 RATE       PIC  V9(3),  VALUE 0.061.
         03 AGE-61-80-RATE       PIC  V9(3),  VALUE 0.079.
         03 AGE-81-99 RATE       PIC  V9(3),  VALUE C.399.
      02 AGE-GROUP-RATE     REDEFINES  AGE-GROUPS-RATES,
                            OCCURS 5 TIMES,  PIC V9(3).
      ...


      IF (APPLICANT-AGE < 21)
             MOVE 1 TO  APPLICANT-AGE-GROUP
      ELSE IF (APPLICANT-AGE < 41)
             MOVE 2 TO  APPLICANT-AGE-GROUP
      ELSE IF (APPLICANT-AGE < 61)
             MOVE 3 TO  APPLICANT-AGE-GROUP
      ELSE IF (APPLICANT-AGE < 81)
             MOVE 4 TO  APPLICANT-AGE-GROUP
      ELSE
             MOVE 5 TO  APPLICANT-AGE-GROUP.

      MOVE  AGE-GROUP-RATE (APPLICANT-AGE-GROUP)
            TO  APPLICANT-INSURANCE-RATE.



   FRAGMENT 2


   01 INSURANCE-RATES-TABLE.
      02 AGES-AND-RATES.
         03 AGE-1-RATE        PIC  V9(3),  VALUE 0.100.
         03 AGE-2-RATE        PIC  V9(3),  VALUE 0.100.
         ...
         03 AGE-20-RATE       PIC  V9(3),  VALUE 0.100.
         03 AGE-21-RATE       PIC  V9(3),  VALUE 0.067.
         03 AGE-22-RATE       PIC  V9(3),  VALUE 0.067.
         ...
         03 AGE-40-RATE       PIC  V9(3),  VALUE C.067.
         03 AGE-41-RATE       PIC  V9(3),  VALUE 0.061.
         03 AGE-42-RATE       PIC  V9(3),  VALUE 0.061.
         ...
         03 AGE-60-RATE       PIC  V9(3),  VALUE 0.061.
         03 AGE-61-RATE       PIC  V9(3),  VALUE 0.079.
         03 AGE-62-RATE       PIC  V9(3),  VALUE 0.079.
         ...
         03 AGE-80-RATE       PIC  V9(3),  VALUE 0.079.
         03 AGE-81-RATE       PIC  V9(3),  VALUE 0.399.
         03 AGE-82-RATE       PIC  V9(3),  VALUE 0.399.
         ...
         03 AGE-99-RATE       PIC  V9(3),  VALUE 0.399.
      02 RATE-FOR-AGE     REDEFINES  AGES-AND-RATES,
                          OCCURS 99 TIMES,  PIC V9(3).
      ...


      MOVE  RATE-FOR-AGE (APPLICANT-AGE)
            TO  APPLICANT-INSURANCE-RATE.
```

Exercise 2.14 (Have Someone Else Read the Work)
Describe two more advantages to having someone else read the work you produce during the various phases of a programming project (see Proverb 17). Describe two disadvantages or bottlenecks.

Exercise 2.15 (Read the Manual Again)
Reread the COBOL manual and find three features that you had forgotten or did not know existed. For each feature give an example of how it would be most useful.

Exercise 2.16 (Guess the Proverb)
What proverb does the program in Example 2.6 violate? (Hint: Assume that you are writing the program.)

Exercise 2.17 (Guess the Proverb)
Consider the following program. Of the 19 programming proverbs, which *single* proverb, if properly followed, would be the most valuable in dealing with the following program?

```
IDENTIFICATION DIVISION.
PROGRAM-ID. "LS-CD".
DATE-WRITTEN.    10/75/6
DATE COMPILED.
ENVIRONMENT DIVISION.
SOURCE-COMPUTER.    IBM-370.
OBJECT-COMPUTER.    IBM-370.
INPUT-OUTPUT SECTION.
FILE-CONTROL.
     SELECT CDFL, ASSIGN TO UR-25HOR-S-CARDFL.
     SELECT PRFL, ASSIGN TO UR-L403-S-LISTING.
DATA DIVISION.
FILE SECTION.
FD  CDFL, LABEL RECORDS OMITTED.
01  CD       PIC A(80).
FD  PRFL, LABEL RECORDS OMITTED.
01  LN       PIC A(80).

PROCEDURE DIVISION.
     OPEN INPUT    CDFL:
     OPEN OUTPUT   PRFL:
READ-FILE.
     READ CDFL   AT END     GOTO   END-ROUTINE:
     WRITE LN FROM CD:
     GOTO   READ-FILE:

END-ROUTINE.
     CLOSE   CDFL,   PRFL:
     STOP:
```

Exercise 2.18 (Using Intermediate Variables)
Usually, a complex mathematical expression can be coded as a single arithmetic expression. However, for the sake of clarity it is often advantageous to split up a lengthy arithmetic expression and use intermediate variables. Give an example where clarity is gained with the use of intermediate variables. Give an example where the obvious result is program efficiency. Give an example where the use of inappropriate or excessive

intermediate variables causes confusion. (Hint: You may want to use Exercise 2.11.)

Exercise 2.19   (Program Organization)

Give two examples where it would be advisable to alphabetize Data Division entries in a section of the Data Division. Also give two examples for procedures in a section of the Procedure Division (see PROC-5 in the Appendix).

Exercise 2.20   (Program Morals)

What is the moral of the following COBOL fragment?

```
02 MY-CUT                  PIC  SV9,     VALUE  0.1.
...
02 FRONT-2-BASE-TAKE       PIC  S9(3),   VALUE  770.
...
02 MY-TAKE                 PIC  S9(2)P.
...


COMPUTE  MY-TAKE  =  MY-CUT * FRONT-2-BASE-TAKE.
```

TOP-DOWN PROGRAMMING

"There is a certain method in this madness."

Horace: *Satires* II.iii

This chapter presents a technique of program development generally known as "top-down programming." The top-down approach presented here is based on the notions of "structured programming" [Ref. D1] and "stepwise refinement" [Ref. W3]. While the technique is not a panacea for all programming ills, it does offer strong guidelines for an intelligent approach to a programming problem.

Before coding, every programmer must develop a complete statement of the problem, a well-planned documentation system, and a clear design strategy. The input format, legal and illegal fields, output files, reports, program messages, and the mapping from all various input data situations to their correct outputs must be described in detail. The documents that need to be produced must also be described, and document timing, writing standards, and library facilities should be established. Furthermore, the overall algorithm also must be determined before coding. It is senseless to start coding a program without such a complete attack on the problem.

Given a solid problem definition and an overall program design, the top-down approach is a method for developing computer programs in any programming language. Although one must be careful to avoid the many pitfalls common to conventional techniques, the top-down approach is one of the major new developments in programming. In brief, the approach has the following characteristics:

1. *Design in Levels.* The programmer designs the program in *levels*, where a level consists of one or more modules. A module is always "complete," although it may reference unwritten submodules. The first level is a complete "main program." A lower level refines or

develops unwritten modules in the upper level. In other words, the modules of a successive level consist of the submodules referenced in the prior level. The programmer may look several levels ahead to determine the best way to design the level at hand.

2. *Initial Language Independence.* The programmer initially uses expressions (often in English) that are relevant to the problem solution, even though the expressions cannot be directly transliterated into COBOL. From statements that are machine and language independent, the programmer moves toward a final machine implementation in COBOL.

3. *Postponement of Details to Lower Levels.* The programmer concentrates on critical broad issues at the initial levels, and postpones details (for example, choice of specific algorithms or intermediate data representations) until lower levels.

4. *Formalization of Each Level.* Before proceeding to a lower level, the programmer ensures that the "program" in its current stage of development is a "formal" statement. In most cases, this means a program that calls unwritten submodules with all arguments spelled out. This step insures that further sections of the program will be developed independently, without having to change the specifications or the interfaces between modules.

5. *Verification of Each Level.* After generating the modules of a new level, the programmer verifies the developing formal statement of the program. This insures that errors pertinent to the current level of development will be detected at their own level.

6. *Successive Refinements.* Each level of the program is refined, formalized, and verified successively until the programmer obtains a completed program that can be transformed easily into COBOL.

One should note several things about the top-down approach. First, the entire problem and its overall solution are presumed to be understood (see Proverbs 2, 3, and 4). It is senseless to start programming until there is a complete understanding of the problem and a complete general plan of attack. Such an understanding allows the programmer to write the program without losing sight of the overall goal.

Second, at the upper levels, the approach is machine and language independent, and the programmer is not constrained by the details of COBOL. He or she is writing the upper levels using a notation that meaningfully solves the problem, although it might not be understood by a COBOL compiler. The programmer's use of a particular notation involves no sacrifice. At each level the statements produced still represent a complete program in some sense. All that is lacking is the machine capable of executing the statements.

Third, at each level of design, informal notation must be formalized as a hypothetical, but explicitly specified, procedure. Specification involves a complete listing of all input and output arguments.

Fourth, at each level the programmer must verify the program in its present form so that further refinements will be absolutely correct with respect to previously designed levels. This ensures that oversights will be detected in their proper context.

For example, suppose that a programmer is working at an intermediate level and generates the following informal statement:

case day-of-the-week *of*
      Monday: generate last week's performance report
      Tuesday: nothing to do
      Wednesday: update personnel file
      Thursday: generate departmental inventory reports
      Friday: generate payroll
      Saturday: nothing to do
      Sunday: nothing to do
  end

The language of this statement is far removed from COBOL. On the other hand, the statement is perfectly clear to the programmer in that it reflects a portion of the desired code. The programmer must elaborate on the required inputs and expected outputs for the procedures, "generate performance report," "update personnel file," "generate inventory reports," and "generate payroll." The next level of refinement must develop each procedure.

The process of solving a problem using the top-down approach can be graphically represented by two trees. The first of them, illustrated in Fig. 3.1, represents the overall program development process. The top-most level, D_0, represents the general conception of the problem. The branches at each succes-

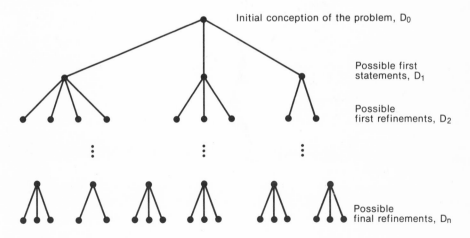

Initial conception of the problem, D_0

Possible first statements, D_1

Possible first refinements, D_2

Possible final refinements, D_n

Fig. 3.1   Overall structure of the top-down programming process

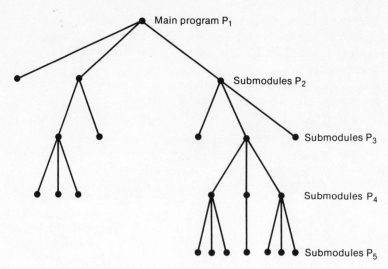

Fig. 3.2   Top-down structure for a specific program

sive level of the tree represent the alternative design decisions that the programmer can make. The paths down the tree represent all possible correct programs
to solve the given problem. The top-down approach allows the programmer to
make design decisions starting from the D_0 level and to follow the tree down-
ward with successive refinements to construct a good solution. At each level the
programmer examines the alternative branches and chooses the one that appears
most suitable. However, if at any time the choice of any branch seems unwise, it
is possible to backtrack up the tree one or more levels and select an alternative
solution. The top-down process for a specific problem is thus a continuous path
of design decisions from D_0 to a specific final program.

The second tree illustrating the top-down approach, shown in Fig. 3.2,
represents the hierarchical structure of a specific program for which five levels
were needed. The top node is the main program, and the nodes at each
successive level are the refined submodules that were introduced but undeveloped in the prior level. By the time the bottom level is reached, we have all the
modules that comprise the final program. An example of such a tree is given
toward the end of this chapter.

There is, of course, a correspondence between the two trees. A single path
from D_0 to a particular design choice in D_n in Fig. 3.1 is expanded and described
in detail in Fig. 3.2.

The top-down approach is a programming technique that can be widely
applied for consistently good results. The technique does not necessarily guarantee the best solution, but it does provide a good structure for solving programming problems. The rest of this chapter will be devoted to an example that
illustrates precisely how the top-down method is used to write well-structured
modular programs. The example also demonstrates that the method is language
independent.

THE ATAD COPPER MINE PROBLEM

General Nicklaus C. Roht, President of the state of Atad, has just purchased a Universal 6 computer for his small country. He has also purchased 100,000 paycheck forms and decides that the first programming job must be the payroll for the country's only industry, the Atad Copper Mine. The General's science advisor, Charles D. Coleman, is placed in charge of the payroll project. Mr. Coleman appoints the state's most experienced system architect, Dr. Irene B. "Top-Down" Malcolm, to be in charge of the major process, the generation of a pay record file and a report to the Copper Mine's operations board.

Irene is uneasy about the fact that General Roht has not yet decided which version of COBOL will become Atad's official programming language. As we shall see, this poses few problems. More important, Irene is disturbed about the following somewhat superficial problem description supplied by Mr. Coleman:

The previous payrolls for the Atad Copper Mine have been handled by an international data processing company that also uses a Universal 6. A weekly work record tape and an up-to-date payroll master tape have been supplied as inputs to the payroll generating program. These inputs are to be kept. They have the following format:

Work Record

Bytes	Meaning
1 → 9	Employee identification number
10 → 13	Regular hours
14 → 17	Overtime hours
18	Bond option ('Y' or 'N')

Master Payroll Record:

Bytes	Meaning
1 → 9	Employee identification number
10 → 39	Employee name
40 → 42	Hourly wage
43 → 44	Number in family
45 → 52	Gross Earnings: Year to date
53 → 59	State taxes: Year to date

The hours worked, hourly wage, earnings, and state tax fields have the normal implied decimal points.

The weekly work records and payroll master records are ordered by ascending value of employee identification number and are correctly created and maintained by separate programs. The program that creates the weekly work record tape also validates each work record.

It is possible for a work record to have an employee identification number not on any master payroll record. Such work records should not be processed but merely punch copied along with an indication of this error.

If a work record is correct, the record should go through the payroll processing. In this case, the program should output a pay record on tape containing the employee's identification number, name and net pay. The net pay is calculated as follows:

$$\text{Net pay} = \text{Gross pay} - \text{State tax} - \text{Bond deduction}$$

where: Gross pay = (hourly wage * regular hours) +
                 (1.5 * hourly wage * overtime hours)
         State tax = (0.25 * Gross pay)/family size
         Bond deduction = $25, if bond option field is 'Y'

There is to be a report generated for the Copper Mine's operations board each time a payroll is processed. The report is simply a list of employees demonstrating a lack of industry or loyalty. General Roht believes that any employee who works less than forty-five total hours or who does not purchase a state bond should be on this list. The operations board will take the proper action concerning those on this list.

Finally, a new payroll master file is to be generated. This is to be identical to the current master file, except that the year-to-date gross earning and state tax fields for each employee are to be updated.

On top of all this, the General insists that the program to generate the pay records and board report be operational five weeks from Friday.

As a summary, a system flowchart has been supplied by Mr. Coleman. This is given in Fig. 3.3.

FUNCTIONAL SPECIFICATION

A professional programmer and a strong advocate of the top-down approach, Irene is calm in the face of General Roht's demands. Despite the fact that a program in an unspecified version of COBOL must be ready in five weeks, she has seen too many programming delays and poor programs caused by a poor problem analysis. Since she is facing a tight schedule, Irene feels all the more that she must revise the given definition and get as complete a functional specification as possible.

The program that Irene must develop maps a work record file and a payroll master file into the corresponding pay record file, board report, illegal work record deck, and updated payroll master file. Before getting into the details of this mapping, Irene first describes as much as she can about the format and contents of these inputs and outputs.

Irene attempts to reconstruct the two program inputs in the form of figures specifying every available detail. While the problem description supplied

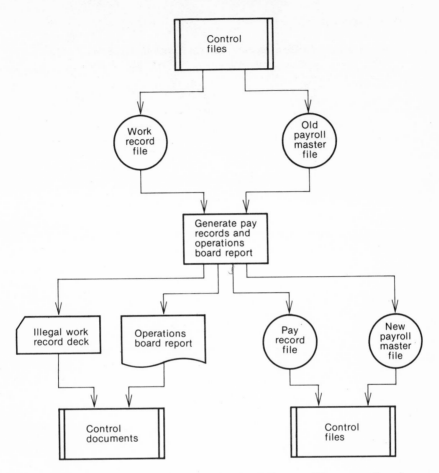

Fig. 3.3 System flowchart for the Atad Copper Mine payroll and report problem

by Mr. Coleman refers to a work record and payroll master record, she realizes that many specifics on the two input files are missing. Starting first with Mr. Coleman, Irene takes immediate action to discover what tape labels are to be used, what the tape blocking factors are, and even whether spaces are allowed in numeric fields. She produces the specifications in Figs. 3.4 and 3.5 after reading through some of the Universal 6 manuals and the available documentation for the processes that generate the input files.

While Irene is specifying the details of the two input files, she notices a number of exceptional input situations not mentioned in the problem definition supplied by Mr. Coleman. It is possible that the labels on the input files are incorrect. It is also possible that an employee payroll record is not matched with an employee work record. Furthermore, it is possible that a work record has

WORK RECORD FILE

Records are ordered on ascending value of ID NUMBER, and the
label consists simply of an ID with value "ACM WEEKLY WORK
RECORDS."

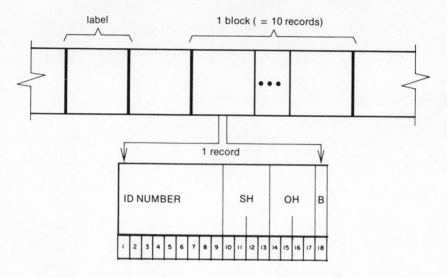

EMPLOYEE WORK RECORD

FIELD	SIZE IN BYTES	CONTENTS
ID NUMBER	9	Integer ⩾ 0 *(No spaces)*
STRAIGHT TIME HOURS (SH)	4	Real Number ⩾ 0 *(Two fractional digits)* *(No spaces)*
OVERTIME HOURS (OH)	4	Real Number ⩾ 0 *(Two fractional digits)* *(No spaces)*
BOND OPTION INDICATION (B)	1	Character ("Y" or "N")

Fig. 3.4   The work record file for the payroll and report problem

zero-valued STRAIGHT TIME HOURS and OVERTIME HOURS, while the
BOND OPTION INDICATION may contain a 'Y'! Irene decides to keep a list of
all such exceptional conditions.

Irene wants to concentrate next on the required outputs for the program,
but she realizes that she had better do something now about a documentation

PAYROLL MASTER FILE

Records are ordered on ascending value of ID NUMBER, and the
label consists of an ID with value "ACM PAYROLL MASTER."

Fig. 3.5 The old and new payroll master files for the payroll and report problem

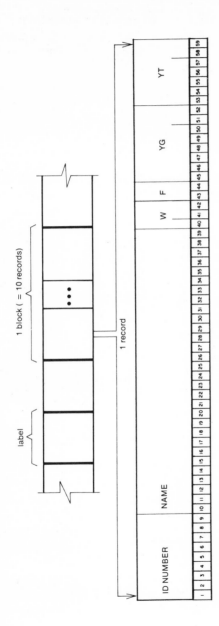

EMPLOYEE PAYROLL RECORD

FIELD	SIZE IN BYTES	CONTENTS
ID NUMBER	9	Integer ≥ 0 *(No spaces)*
NAME	30	Alphabetic Name *(Last, First, M.I.)* *(Left justified)* *(Spaces separate name components)*
FAMILY SIZE (F)	2	Integer ≥ 1 *(No spaces)*

FIELD	SIZE IN BYTES	CONTENTS
HOURLY WAGE (W)	3	Real Number > 0 *(Two fractional digits)* *(No spaces)*
YEAR TO DATE GROSS PAY (YG)	8	Real Number ≥ 0 *(Two fractional digits)* *(No spaces)*
YEAR TO DATE TAXES (YT)	7	Real Number ≥ 0 *(Two fractional digits)* *(No spaces)*

system. Since she is on a tight schedule, the documentation policy must be made simple. Irene decides that when she completes the problem definition work, she will write a short introduction, attach the results of her functional specification and system flowchart from Mr. Coleman, and use it to describe the entire system as seen by the user: Volume 1 of the program documentation. Furthermore, there will be only two other volumes in the documentation set: a program description (Volume 2) and an operator's manual (Volume 3). She will, of course, provide a cross reference index. Irene plans to use the various levels of the top-down approach as the basis for the program description. The operator's manual will consist of a short description of operating procedures and an explanation of program messages. Irene plans to write the second and third volumes as she progresses through the top-down approach.

Irene now feels comfortable enough to specify the required outputs from the program. As for the pay record file, there are few problems. The documentation for the process which is to print the weekly payroll checks provides Irene with the needed information. The pay record NET PAY field is large enough to accommodate any possible net pay value. However, while thinking about the employees' electing the bond option, she also uncovers another exceptional problem condition involving employees who have not earned enough to cover the cost of a desired bond. Irene adds this condition to her exceptional condition list. By lunch time of the next day, Irene finishes the details of the format and contents of the pay records output. Her results are given in Fig. 3.6.

Upon returning from lunch, Irene next attacks the specification of the report to the operations board. Irene decides that it would be nice to print a line that gives the total number of disloyal employees at the end of the list. She meets with the head of the operations board to discuss the desired report layout and her ideas. After much discussion and output field size estimates, a consensus on the report content and the layout of Fig. 3.7 is reached. During the discussion, Irene notes more exceptional situations. First, sick leave is not condoned and vacations are not allowed at the Atad Copper Mine, and thus absent employees are to be put on the disloyal list. In fact, a disloyal employee is any employee for whom a pay record is not produced. Second, when there are no disloyal employees, the board report consists of just two pages, with page 2 having the summation line on line 14. Third, because the Atad Copper Mine is a relatively small operation (only 4096 employees at present), it is unlikely that the capacity of PAGE NUMBER or NUMBER DISLOYAL would ever be exceeded.

Just as she is finishing the executive report specifications, a new programmer, Dorothy E. Clark, drops in and notices the amount of work Irene is faced with. "Why are you bothering with all this?" she asks. "In college, I was told to try to keep things as short and simple as possible." Irene replies that any evident complexity was not introduced by her but exists in the problem itself. The painstaking definition of the payroll and report problem will not be perfect (what is?), but it will be so close that it is unlikely that programming changes will have to be made later during top-down development or coding. Irene also

PAY RECORD FILE

Records are ordered on ascending value of ID NUMBER, and the label consists simply of an ID with value "ACM PAY RECORDS."

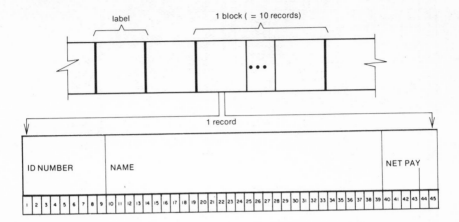

EMPLOYEE PAY RECORD

FIELD	SIZE IN BYTES	CONTENTS
ID NUMBER	9	Integer ≥ 0 (No spaces)
NAME	30	Alphabetic Name (Last, first, M.I.) (Left justified) (Spaces separate name components)
NET PAY	6	Real Number ≥ 0 (Two fractional digits) (No spaces

MAJOR FORMULAS (All results are rounded)

NET PAY = GROSS PAY − STATE TAX − BOND DEDUCTION

GROSS PAY = (HOURLY WAGE * STRAIGHT TIME HOURS)
        + (1.5 *HOURLY WAGE * OVERTIME HOURS)

STATE TAX = (0.25 * GROSS PAY)/ FAMILY SIZE

BOND DEDUCTION = 25, *if* BOND OPTION INDICATION = "Y"
             0, *if* BOND OPTION INDICATION = "N"

Fig. 3.6 The pay record file for the payroll and report problem

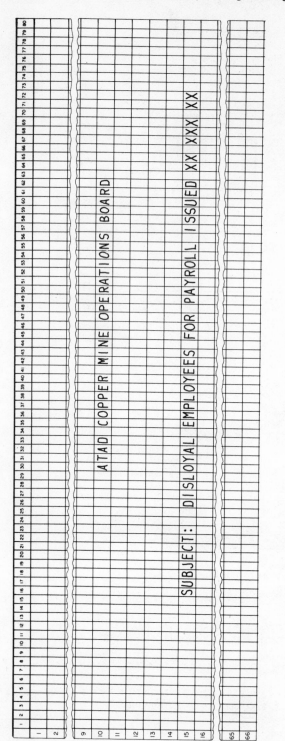

COVER PAGE

FIELD	LINE	CONTENTS
DATE	15	Date in standard format (e.g. 75 AUG 05)

Fig. 3.7a   Operations Board Report: Cover page

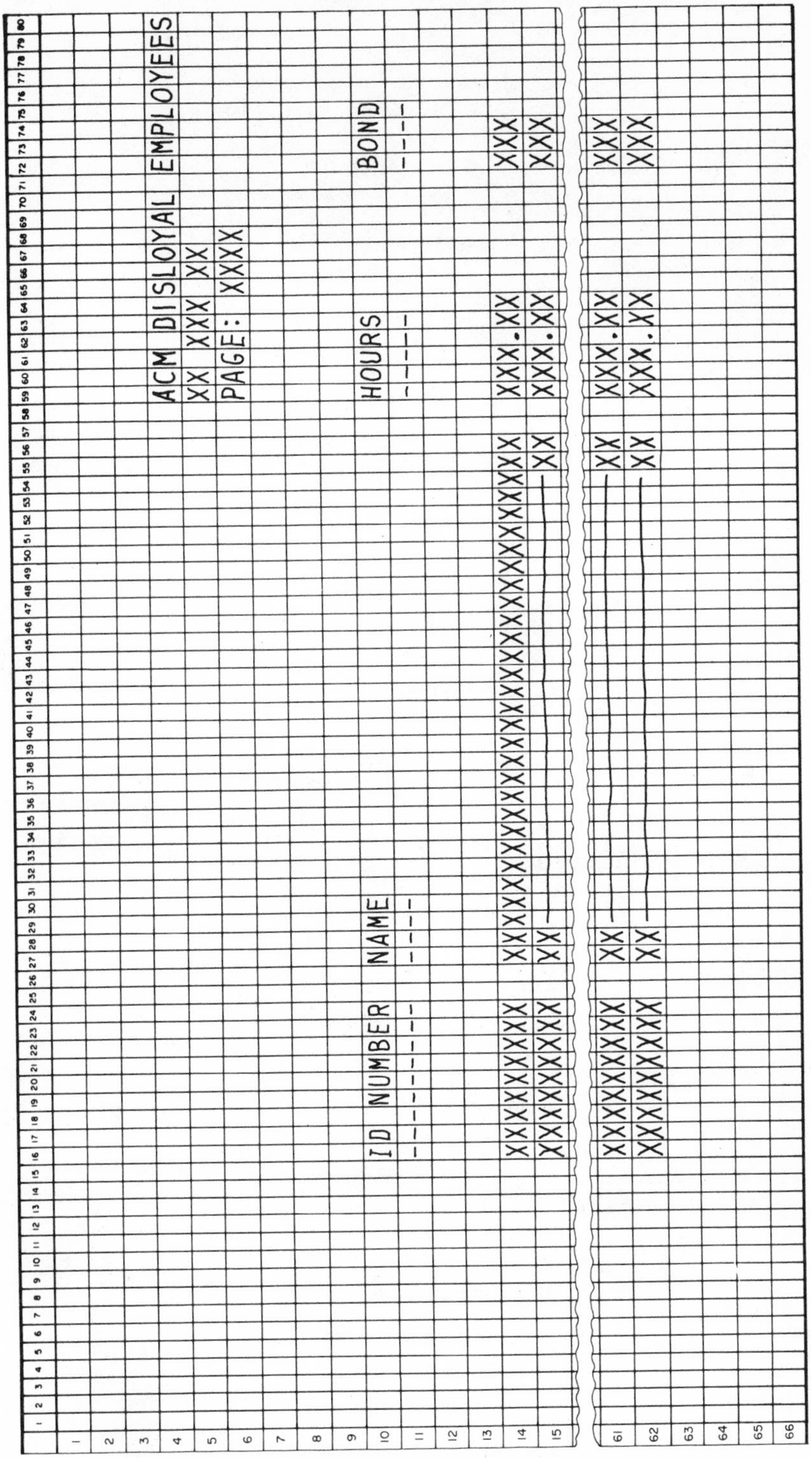

ACM DISLOYAL EMPLOYEES
XX XXX XX
PAGE:: XXXX

ID NUMBER NAME   HOURS   BOND

XXXXXXXX XXXXXXXXXXXXXXXXXXXXXXXXXX   XXX.XX   XXX
XXXXXXXX XX   XXX.XX   XXX

Fig. 3.7b   Operations Board Report: Successive pages (see next page)

SUCCESSIVE PAGES

FIELD	LINE	CONTENTS
DATE	5	Date in standard format
PAGE NUMBER	6	Integer ⩾ 2 *(Leading zeros suppressed)*
ID NUMBER	14–62	Integer ⩾ 0 *(No spaces)*
NAME	14–62	Alphabetic name *(Last, first, M.I.)* *(Left justified)* *(Spaces separate name components)*
TOTAL HOURS WORKED	14–62	200.00 > Real Number ⩾ 0.0 *(Hundreds and tens position zeros suppressed)*
BOND PURCHASE INDICATION	14–62	Character *("YES" or "NO")* *(Left justified)*

Fig 3.7b (cont'd)

SUMMATION LINE

FIELD	LINE	CONTENTS
NUMBER DISLOYAL	Three lines after end of disloyal employees list, or on line 14 of Page 2.	Integer ⩾ 0 *(Leading zeros suppressed)* *("0" when zero)*

Fig. 3.7c   Operations Board Report: Summation line

points out that thinking now will not only save time later but, more important, will help produce the desired program. In addition, the meticulous functional specification will describe the system as seen by the user (Volume 1 of the documentation).

There are only two more outputs for the payroll problem. One is the new payroll master tape. The format and contents of this output are the same as that for the input payroll master tape given in Figure 3.5. The other remaining output is the illegal work record deck. The format and contents of a card in this deck are the same as those of an input work record (see Figure 3.4), with the exception that an error message is attached indicating why the work record is illegal.

In forming the specification for the illegal work record deck, Irene realizes that there is a temptation not to bother creating the actual error messages now. Nevertheless, the specification of error messages is a crucial task since it causes the programmer to summarize the exceptions that must be looked for by the eventual program. Later patching of a program in order to meet missed exceptions can be quite disrupting and expensive.

Irene carefully reviews the original problem specification from Mr. Coleman, analyzes her input and output forms, and looks at her list of exceptional conditions. All this information establishes the following three conditions under which an input work record is copied into the illegal work record deck.

1. The old payroll master file does not contain an entry corresponding to the work record.
2. The work record has fields STRAIGHT TIME HOURS and OVER-TIME HOURS both zero valued.
3. The cost of a desired bond cannot be met.

Irene decides on a simple error notation format where one of three suitable messages will be punched beginning in column 31 for any illegal work record. She appends the possible messages to the specification, thereby yielding the complete specification of the illegal work record deck in Figure 3.8.

Having completed the detailing of the format and contents of the various inputs and outputs, Irene now describes the function that maps an input configuration for the payroll and report problem into an output response. Such a description is invaluable to the programmer who develops the eventual program. Irene's description in Figure 3.9 consists of nested conditions that describe output responses to each input situation.

Irene is exhausted after the writing of the functional specification. Since it is almost 5 o'clock anyway, she decides to leave early for a weekend conference dealing with advances in programming language.

When Irene returns on Monday morning, she is notified of a call from Mr. Coleman last Friday afternoon. She contacts Mr. Coleman, who is anxious to know how the program is progressing. Irene informs him everything is on schedule, and she should have Volume 1 of the documentation to him the day after tomorrow, news that Mr. Coleman is pleased to hear.

Ignoring the mounting pressure, Irene decides to complete the functional specification by listing all programs implementation requirements that will be followed. First, a top-down development of the program will be performed. Second, since the Universal 6 will come with a virtual memory based operating

ID NUMBER	SH	OH	B	FILL	REASON ILLEGAL
1 2 3 4 5 6 7 8 9	10 11 12 13	14 15 16 17	18	19 20 21 22 23 24 25 26 27 28 29 30	31 32 33 34 35 36 • • • 77 78 79 80

ILLEGAL WORK RECORD DECK

Records are ordered on ascending value of ID NUMBER. The record format is:

ILLEGAL EMPLOYEE WORK RECORD

FIELD	SIZE IN BYTES	CONTENTS
ID NUMBER	9	Integer ⩾ 0 *(No spaces)*
STRAIGHT TIME HOURS (SH)	4	Real Number ⩾ 0 *(Two fractional digits)* *(No spaces)*
OVERTIME HOURS (OH)	4	Real Number ⩾ 0 *(Two fractional digits)* *(No spaces)*
BOND OPTION INDICATION (B)	1	Character *('Y' or 'N')*
FILL	12	Spaces
REASON ILLEGAL	50	Error Message *(Left justified)* *(See below)*

ERROR MESSAGE FORMS

1. *** NO PAYROLL MASTER RECORD FOR THIS EMPLOYEE
2. *** HOURS FIELDS BOTH ZERO
3. *** CANNOT MEET BOND COST

Fig. 3.8 The illegal work record deck for the payroll and report problem

system, and since the program is on a very tight schedule, no time should be wasted to produce short, fast running code beyond what can be achieved from sensible upper level design. Third, since the actual COBOL compiler version is not known at this time, all COBOL code should conform to the ANSI-74 standard. In fact, all coding should be as simple and direct as possible. Fourth,

Condition 1   Either of the two input files is missing or incorrectly labeled.
Action   Let the system generate an error message.
Condition 2   Both input files are correctly labeled.
  Condition 2.1   Both input files are empty.
  Action   Display the following message to the system operator.
*** FROM ACM WEEKLY PAYROLL AND BOARD REPORT PROGRAM:
    BOTH INPUT FILES ARE EMPTY.
    EXECUTION ABORTION. NO OUTPUTS PRODUCED.
Condition 2.2   The work record file is not empty, but the old payroll master
    file is.
  Action   Display the following message to the system operator.
*** FROM ACM WEEKLY PAYROLL AND BOARD REPORT PROGRAM:
    THE INPUT PAYROLL MASTER FILE IS EMPTY.
    EXECUTION ABORTED. NO OUTPUTS PRODUCED
Condition 2.3   The old payroll master file is not empty, but the work record
    file is.
  Action   Display the following message to the system operator.
*** FROM ACM WEEKLY PAYROLL AND BOARD REPORT PROGRAM:
    THE INPUT WORK RECORD FILE IS EMPTY.
    EXECUTION ABORTED. NO OUTPUTS PRODUCED.
Condition 2.4   Both input files are not empty.
  Action   Generate the new payroll master file according to the
    following rules.
    Condition 2.4.1   There are old payroll master records having no
      matching legal work record. (See Figure 3.8)
    Action   Copy each such old payroll master record as a new
      payroll master record.
    Condition 2.4.2   There are old payroll master records having a
      matching legal work record.
    Action   Copy each such old payroll master record as a new
      payroll master record, updating the YEAR TO
      DATE GROSS PAY and YEAR TO DATE TAXES
      fields.
  Action   Generate the pay record file or system operator message
    according to the following rules.
    Condition 2.4.3   There are no legal work records.
    Action   Do not generate the pay record file.
    Action   Display the following message to the system
      operator.
*** FROM ACM WEEKLY PAYROLL AND BOARD REPORT PROGRAM:
    THE INPUT WORK RECORD FILE CONTAINS ALL ILLEGAL
    RECORDS.

*Fig. 3.9 Mapping of input situations to output responses for the
payroll and report problem*

THE OUTPUT PAY RECORD FILE WAS NOT PRODUCED.

Condition 2.4.4 There is at least one legal work record.

Action   Use each legal work record and matching old payroll master record to create a pay record.

Action Generate the illegal work record deck or system operator message according to the following rules.

Condition 2.4.5 There is at least one illegal input work record.

Action   Copy each work record that is illegal to an illegal work record card, appending the appropriate error message.

Condition 2.4.6 There are no illegal input work records.

Action   Do not generate illegal work record deck.

Action   Display the following message to the system operator.

*** FROM ACM WEEKLY PAYROLL AND BOARD REPORT PROGRAM: ALL RECORDS IN THE WORK RECORD FILE ARE LEGAL. THE OUTPUT ILLEGAL WORK RECORD DECK WAS NOT PRODUCED.

Action Generate the operations board report according to the following rules.

Condition 2.4.7 There are no disloyal employees.

Action   Produce the summation line on line 14 of page two of the operations board report. (See Figure 3.7)

Condition 2.4.8 There is at least one disloyal employee.

Action   For each employee having no matching legal input work record, generate a disloyal employee line with TOTAL HOURS WORKED containing zero and BOND PURCHASE INDICATION containing "NO".

Action   For each employee having a matching legal input work record but who has worked under 45 hours or has not purchased a state bond, generate a disloyal employee line that reports the hours worked and whether a state bond was purchased.

Action   Produce the summation line that follows the listing of disloyal employees and indicates the size of that listing.

Fig 3.9   Mapping of Input situations (cont'd)

and very important, the new Atad Copper Mine COBOL program standards (given in Chapter 4) will be followed. Fifth and last, Save-Restart considerations can be ignored.

The functional specification of user requirements is done! Irene happily restructures her results, and along with the system flowchart, a security and authorization analysis, and a brief introduction, she collects them into a draft of the Volume 1 documentation manual. A copy is sent to Mr. Coleman. Irene drops off other copies to the head of the operations board and one or two of her colleagues for quick but careful review. Top-down development cannot begin until all criticisms or problems are disposed of.

TOP-DOWN PROGRAM DEVELOPMENT

Irene is becoming involved with the management of the payroll and report programming project and must also begin organizing the remaining volumes of the documentation set. Irene decides to bring in Dorothy Clark to do the actual top-down development of the payroll and report program.

When Irene meets with Dorothy, she explains that since the payroll and report problem is straightforward, the programming should not be too difficult. The problem is fully specified. Moreover, as a part of normal practice, she tells Dorothy that they will work together closely at the beginning of the top-down development. Irene gives Dorothy a copy of the draft functional specification of user requirements and a brief exposition of the top-down approach to programming. Irene asks Dorothy to give these a careful reading and return the day after next to begin the actual work.

When Dorothy returns, she surprises Irene with the following initial top-down development of the program, P_1:

P_1 (First pass)

check the input files
if either input file is missing *or* is labeled incorrectly
then let operating system generate error message
else if either input file is empty
      then write appropriate message to system console
      else prepare for payroll and report generation
          generate payroll and report
          clean up after generation
stop

Irene is pleased with a good attempt but notes a few of its problems. First, Dorothy's P_1 contains a specification of processing actions but no mention of the data to be manipulated. Second, Dorothy checks for empty input files but fails to mention that this is done by reading both files. Third, "generate payroll and report" is a nebulous procedure, one that even Dorothy will admit is in need of formalization. And why compound the problem by associating it with two other vague procedures, "prepare for payroll and report generation" and "clean up after generation." Together, Irene and Dorothy settle on the following informal main program of the payroll and report program:

P₁ (Informal): Produce ACM payroll and report
describe input and output files
open files and check labels
read a payroll record
read a work record
if either read attempt indicates an empty file
    then write appropriate message to system console
    else produce payroll and report
stop

Irene points out that it is a good idea to keep the initial attempt at writing a level of the program informal, because it makes it easier to understand the total picture. However, the level must be formalized and verified before any thought of further refinement. The essential idea behind formalization is to distinguish between something that is vague and something that is merely undeveloped. Formalizing usually entails spelling out all implicit data items and how each construct uses them. Formalizing is also a matter of verification, since errors and omissions are usually picked up in the process. Irene works hard with Dorothy to develop the final formalized main program P₁. Irene and Dorothy carefully review P₁ and find no mistakes.

P₁ (Formal): Produce ACM payroll and report

describe files (OLD-PAYROLL-MASTER-FILE, WORK-REC-FILE,
    NEW-PAYROLL-MASTER-FILE, OPERATIONS-BOARD-RPT,
    PAY-REC-FILE, ILLEGAL-WORK-REC-DECK)

open files and check labels OLD-PAYROLL-MASTER-FILE,
    WORK-REC-FILE
read an EMPL-PAYROLL-REC from OLD-PAYROLL-MASTER-FILE.
read an EMPL-WORK-REC from WORK-REC-FILE.

select the appropriate action.
    if (OLD-PAYROLL-MASTER-FILE *and* WORK-REC-FILE are empty)
        then write program message to systen console. (See condition 2.1
        in condition-action list)
    if (OLD-PAYROLL-MASTER-FILE is empty *but* WORK-REC-FILE is
        not empty)
        then write program message to system console. (See condition 2.2)
    if (OLD-PAYROLL-MASTER-FILE is not empty *but*
        WORK-REC-FILE is empty)
        then write program message to system console. (See condition 2.3)
    if (OLD-PAYROLL-MASTER-FILE *and* WORK-REC-FILE are not
        empty)

then produce payroll and report
    —using for input EMPL-PAYROLL-REC,
       EMPL-WORK-REC, OLD-PAYROLL-MASTER-FILE,
       WORK-REC-FILE
    —possibly outputting PAY-REC-FILE, OPERATIONS-
       BOARD-RPT, NEW-PAYROLL-MASTER-FILE,
       IILLEGAL-WORK-REC-DECK, (Console messages)

close files OLD-PAYROLL-MASTER-FILE, WORK-REC-FILE
stop

Since Dorothy seems to have the idea now, Irene asks her to refine the procedure, "produce payroll and report," which they both agree is about all there is in P_1 in need of refinement. They will get together to formalize and verify the resulting P_2 the next day.

The following informal version, P_2, of the submodule "produce payroll and report" is the result of Dorothy's labor.

P_2 (Informal): Produce payroll and report

describe report variables
open files and write labels
initialize board report

repeat the following
    compare and process input records
until (OLD-PAYROLL-MASTER-FILE *or* WORK-REC-FILE is empty)

if (OLD-PAYROLL-MASTER-FILE is not empty)
    then repeat the following
        process unmatched master record
       read next EMPL-PAYROLL-REC
    until (OLD-PAYROLL-MASTER-FILE empty)
if (WORK-REC-FILE is not empty)
    then repeat the following
        process unmatched work record
       read next EMPL-WORK-REC
    until (WORK-REC-FILE empty)
produce board report summation line
if (PAY-REC-FILE is empty)
    then write program message to system console
if (ILLEGAL-WORK-REC-DECK is empty)
    then write program message to system console

close files and write labels
return

Irene is pleased with the result, especially with its clarity. Dorothy mentions that the biggest problem was maintaining a high level of abstraction while not worrying about too much at one time. Dorothy's first pass at P_2 ran three pages. Dorothy mentions also that she has looked ahead and anticipates using the COBOL Report Writer. Together, Dorothy and Irene formalize and verify the module in P_2, as follows:

P_2 (Formal): Produce payroll and report

describe NUM-DISLOYAL-EMPL, SIZE-PAY-REC-FILE,
          SIZE-ILLEGAL-WORK-REC-DECK

open files and write labels PAY-REC-FILE, OPERATIONS-BOARD-RPT,
          NEW-PAYROLL-MASTER-FILE, ILLEGAL-WORK-REC-DECK
get ANSI date
    —outputting TODAYS-DATE
initialize board report
    —using for input TODAYS-DATE
NUM-DISLOYAL-EMPL = 0
SIZE-PAY-REC-FILE = 0
SIZE-ILLEGAL-WORK-REC-DECK = 0

repeat the following
        compare and process input records
        —using for input OLD-PAYROLL-MASTER-FILE,
                WORK-REC-FILE, old EMPL-PAYROLL-REC,
                EMPL-WORK-REC, NUM-DISLOYAL-EMPL,
                SIZE-PAY-REC-FILE,
                SIZE-ILLEGAL-WORK-REC-DECK
        —possibly outputting EMPL-PAY-REC,
                DISLOYAL-EMPL-LINE, new EMPL-PAYROLL-REC,
                ILLEGAL-EMPL-WORK-REC,
                NUM-DISLOYAL-EMPL, SIZE-PAY-REC-FILE,
                SIZE-ILLEGAL-WORK-REC-DECK, next old
                EMPL-PAYROLL-REC, next EMPL-WORK-REC
until (OLD-PAYROLL-MASTER-FILE *or* WORK-REC-FILE empty)

if (OLD-PAYROLL-MASTER-FILE not empty)
    then repeat the following
            process unmatched master record
            —using for input old EMPL-PAYROLL-REC,
                    NUM-DISLOYAL-EMPL
            —outputting DISLOYAL-EMPL-LINE,
                    new EMPL-PAYROLL-REC,
                    NUM-DISLOYAL-EMPL
        read next EMPL-PAYROLL-REC from

OLD-PAYROLL-MASTER-FILE
        until (OLD-PAYROLL-MASTER-FILE empty)
if (WORK-REC-FILE not empty)
        then repeat the following
            process unmatched work record.
                —using for input EMPL-WORK-REC,
                    SIZE-ILLEGAL-WORK-REC-DECK
                —outputting ILLEGAL-EMPL-WORK-REC,
                    SIZE-ILLEGAL-WORK-REC-DECK
            read next EMPL-WORK-REC
        until (WORK-REC-FILE empty)

generate summation line
        —using for input NUM-DISLOYAL-EMPL
if SIZE-PAY-REC-FILE = 0
        then write program message to system console (see condition 2.4.3 of
            condition-action list)
if SIZE-ILLEGAL-WORK-REC-DECK = 0
        then write program message to system console (see condition 2.4.6)

terminate board report
close files PAY-REC-FILE, OPERATIONS-BOARD-RPT,
            NEW-PAYROLL-MASTER-FILE, ILLEGAL-WORK-REC-DECK
return

The module "produce payroll and report" requires the refinement of four modules. As an aid in keeping track of the structure of the developing program, Irene sketches the tree diagram of Figure 3.10. One of the modules, "get ANSI date," has already been written for another programming project.

Dorothy now seems to understand the top-down approach fully. Irene tells her to finish the entire program, cautioning her to recall the program implementation requirements. Irene will, of course, be available to help with any problems that arise. Irene recommends to Dorothy that she should code upper level modules whenever lower level refinement becomes tedious. This will also allow Irene to get Herman I. Stone of the Government Data Services Center to manage the inputting of the actual code as soon as possible. And yes, of course, Mr. Coleman would be delighted to hear how many lines of code have been produced.

The story of Irene and Dorothy ends here. In a matter of another week and a half, they completed coding the payroll and report program that is given in Example 3.1. (Example 3.2 contains the available COBOL library texts that were conveniently copied.) The program quickly passed initial shakedown testing, and the authors were very optimistic about the upcoming formal test phase. To be truthful, the program was a little behind schedule, but all in all they surprised many in the State of Atad.

Example 3.1   Final Payroll and Report Program

```
IDENTIFICATION DIVISION.

    PROGRAM-ID.
    PRODUCE-ACM-PAYROLL-AND-RPT.

    AUTHOR.
    DOROTHY E. CLARK  AND  DR. IRENE B. MALCOLM.

    INSTALLATION.
    PROGRAMMING PROVERBS INSTITUTE,  STATE OF ATAD.

    DATE-COMPILED.
    76 JAN 28.

    SECURITY.
    THIS PROGRAM MUST BE RUN WITH AN OLD-PAYROLL-MASTER-FILE AND
    WORK-REC-FILE GENERATED FOR THE CURRENT WEEKLY PAYROLL.

*     **    THE TASK PERFORMED BY THIS PROGRAM IS
*     **    DESCRIBED IN VOLUME ONE OF THE ACM PAYROLL
*     **    AND REPORT DOCUMENTATION SET.  THIS PROGRAM
*     **    IS DESCRIBED IN DETAIL IN VOLUME TWO OF THAT
*     **    SAME SET:  A BRIEF DESCRIPTION FOLLOWS.

*     **    FOR INPUT THIS PROGRAM EXPECTS TWO FILES.
*     **       OLD-PAYROLL-MASTER-FILE:  A SEQUENCE OF
*     **          EMPLOYEE PAYROLL MASTER RECORDS ORDERED BY
*     **          ASCENDING VALUE OF EMPLOYEE ID NUMBER.
*     **       WORK-REC-FILE:  A SEQUENCE OF EMPLOYEE
*     **          WEEKLY WORK RECORDS ORDERED BY
*     **          ASCENDING VALUE OF EMPLOYEE ID NUMBER.
*     **
*     **    AS NORMAL OUTPUT THIS PROGRAM PRODUCES FOUR FILES.
*     **       NEW-PAYROLL-MASTER-FILE:  AN UPDATED COPY OF THE
*     **          OLD-PAYROLL-MASTER-FILE REFLECTING THE WEEKLY
*     **          PAYROLL.
*     **       PAY-REC-FILE:  A SEQUENCE OF PAY  RECORDS
*     **          ORDERED BY ASCENDING VALUE OF
*     **          EMPLOYEE ID NUMBER.
*     **       OPERATIONS-BOARD-RPT:  A LISTING OF ALL EMPLOYEES
*     **          WHO DID NOT GET PAID, WORKED FEWER THAN THE
*     **          EXPECTED MINIMUM HOURS, OR DID NOT PURCHASE
*     **          A STATE BOND.
*     **       ILLEGAL-WORK-REC-DECK:  AN ANNOTATED COPY OF EACH
*     **          EMPLOYEE WORK RECORD NOT SATISFYING NORMAL
*     **          PROCESSING REQUIREMENTS.
*     **
*     **    AS ABNORMAL OUTPUT THIS PROGRAM PRODUCES SYSTEM CONSOLE
*     **    MESSAGES EXPLAINING IRREGULARITIES WITH ONE OR MORE
*     **    INPUT OR OUTPUT FILES.
```

```
ENVIRONMENT DIVISION.

CONFIGURATION SECTION.

    SOURCE-COMPUTER.
    UNIVERSAL-6 WITH DEBUGGING MODE.

    OBJECT-COMPUTER.
    UNIVERSAL-6.

    SPECIAL-NAMES.
    LINE-PTR-02 IS VERIFICATION-PRINTER.


INPUT-OUTPUT SECTION.

    FILE-CONTROL.
    SELECT OLD-PAYROLL-MASTER-FILE
        ASSIGN TO TAPE-UNIT-01.
    SELECT WORK-REC-FILE
        ASSIGN TO TAPE-UNIT-02.
    SELECT PAY-REC-FILE
        ASSIGN TO TAPE-UNIT-03.
    SELECT OPERATIONS-BOARD-RPT
        ASSIGN TO LINE-PTR-01.
    SELECT NEW-PAYROLL-MASTER-FILE
        ASSIGN TO TAPE-UNIT-04.
    SELECT ILLEGAL-WORK-REC-DECK
        ASSIGN TO CARD-PCH-01.
```

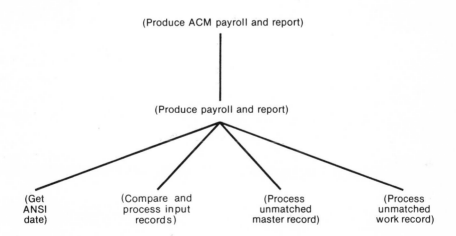

Fig. 3.10 The initial structure of the program, "Produce ACM
payroll and report"

```
DATA DIVISION.

FILE SECTION.

    COPY  FD-ACM-PAYROLL-MASTER-FILE
      REPLACING  PAYROLL-MASTER-FILE   BY   OLD-PAYROLL-MASTER-FILE.

    COPY  FD-ACM-WORK-REC-FILE.

    COPY  FD-ACM-PAYROLL-MASTER-FILE
      REPLACING  PAYROLL-MASTER-FILE   BY   NEW-PAYROLL-MASTER-FILE.

    COPY  FD-ACM-PAY-REC-FILE.

    FD  OPERATIONS-BOARD-RPT
          LABEL RECORDS OMITTED,
          REPORT IS  BOARD-RPT.

    FD  ILLEGAL-WORK-REC-DECK
          LABEL RECORDS OMITTED.
    01  ILLEGAL-WORK-REC-CARD.
        02 ID-NUM                  PIC  9(9).
        02 STRAIGHT-TIME-HOURS      PIC  9(2)V9(2).
        02 OVERTIME-HOURS           PIC  9(2)V9(2).
        02 BOND-OPTION-INDICATION   PIC  X(1).
        02 FILLER                   PIC  X(12).
        02 REASON-ILLEGAL           PIC  X(50).
```

```
WORKING-STORAGE  SECTION.

01 BOARD-RPT-INFO.
   02 TODAYS-DATE                        PIC  X(9).
   02 NUM-DISLOYAL-EMPL                  PIC  9(6).
   02 DISLOYAL-EMPL-LINE-ITEMS.
      03 ID-NUM                          PIC  9(9).
      03 NAME                            PIC  X(30).
      03 TOTAL-HOURS-WORKED              PIC  9(3)V9(2).
      03 BOND-PURCHASE-INDICATION        PIC  X(3).
   02 BOND-BOUGHT-INDICATION            PIC  X(3),  VALUE  "YES".
   02 NO-BOND-BOUGHT-INDICATION         PIC  X(3),  VALUE  "NO".
   02 EXPECTED-MINIMUM-HOURS            PIC  9(2)V9(2),  VALUE 45.00.

01 FILE-STATUS-INFO.
   02 OLD-PAYROLL-MASTER-FILE-STATUS       PIC 9(1).
      88 EOF-OLD-PAYROLL-MASTER-FILE            VALUE 1.
   02 WORK-REC-FILE-STATUS                  PIC 9(1).
      88 EOF-WORK-REC-FILE                      VALUE 1.
   02 SIZE-PAY-REC-FILE                     PIC  9(6).
      88 EMPTY-PAY-REC-FILE                     VALUE 0.
   02 SIZE-ILLEGAL-WORK-REC-DECK            PIC  9(6).
      88 EMPTY-ILLEGAL-WORK-REC-DECK            VALUE 0.

01 ILLEGAL-WORK-REC-DECK-INFO.
   02 REASON-WORK-REC-ILLEGAL            PIC  X(50).
   02 UNMATCHED-MSG                      PIC  X(50),  VALUE
         "*** NO PAYROLL MASTER RECORD FOR THIS EMPLOYEE".
   02 ZERO-TOTAL-HOURS-MSG               PIC  X(50),
         VALUE  "*** HOURS FIELDS BOTH ZERO".
   02 CANT-AFFORD-BOND-MSG               PIC  X(50),
         VALUE  "*** CANNOT MEET BOND COST".

01 PAY-REC-FILE-INFO.
   02 STD-BOND-DEDUCTION                 PIC  9(2)V9(2),  VALUE 25.00.
   02 OVERTIME-FACTOR                    PIC  9V9(2),  VALUE 1.5.
   02 STATE-TAX-RATE                     PIC  V9(2),  VALUE 0.25.
   02 CALC-ITEMS.
      03 TOTAL-HOURS-WORKED              PIC  9(3)V9(2).
      03 STRAIGHT-TIME-PAY               PIC  9(4)V9(2).
      03 OVERTIME-PAY                    PIC  9(4)V9(2).
      03 GROSS-PAY                       PIC  9(4)V9(2).
      03 STATE-TAX                       PIC  9(4)V9(2).
      03 BOND-DEDUCTION                  PIC  9(2)V9(2).
      03 BEFORE-BOND-PAY                 PIC  9(4)V9(2).
      03 NET-PAY                         PIC  9(4)V9(2).
      03 NET-PAY-CALC-CONDITION          PIC  9(1).
         88 BOND-NOT-AFFORDABLE              VALUE 1.
```

```
01 PROGRAM-MSG-INFO.
   02 PROGRAM-MSG                 PIC X(72).
   02 INTRO-MSG                   PIC X(72), VALUE
      "*** FROM ACM WEEKLY PAYROLL AND BOARD REPORT PROGRAM:".
   02 EMPTY-INPUTS-MSG            PIC X(72), VALUE
      "     BOTH INPUT FILES ARE EMPTY.".
   02 ABORT-MSG                   PIC X(72), VALUE
      "     EXECUTION ABORTED.  NO OUTPUTS PRODUCED.".
   02 EMPTY-OLD-MASTER-MSG        PIC X(72), VALUE
      "     THE INPUT PAYROLL MASTER FILE IS EMPTY.".
   02 EMPTY-WORK-MSG              PIC X(72), VALUE
      "     THE INPUT WORK RECORD FILE IS EMPTY.".
   02 NO-LEGAL-WORK-RECS-MSG      PIC X(72), VALUE
      "     THE INPUT WORK RECORD FILE CONTAINS ALL ILLEGAL R
      "ECORDS.".
   02 EMPTY-PAY-MSG               PIC X(72), VALUE
      "     THE OUTPUT PAY RECORD FILE WAS NOT PRODUCED.".
   02 ALL-LEGAL-WORK-RECS-MSG     PIC X(72), VALUE
      "     ALL RECORDS IN THE INPUT WORK RECORD FILE ARE LEG
      "AL.".
   02 EMPTY-ILLEGAL-DECK-MSG      PIC X(72), VALUE
      "     THE OUTPUT ILLEGAL WORK RECORD DECK WAS NOT PRODU
      "CED.".

01 VERIFICATION-INFO.
   02 LOG-HEADER                  PIC X(120), VALUE
      "          *** VERIFICATION OF PRODUCE-ACM-PAYROLL-AND
      "-RPT ***".
   02 PRE-WARN-EMPTY-INPUTS-MSG   PIC X(120), VALUE
      "- PERFORMING WARN-OF-EMPTY-INPUTS".
   02 PRE-WARN-EMPTY-MASTER-MSG   PIC X(120), VALUE
      "- PERFORMING WARN-OF-EMPTY-OLD-MASTER".
   02 PRE-WARN-EMPTY-WORK-MSG     PIC X(120), VALUE
      "- PERFORMING WARN-OF-EMPTY-WORK".
   02 PRE-PRODUCE-PAYROLL-MSG     PIC X(120), VALUE
      "- PERFORMING PRODUCE-PAYROLL-AND-RPT".
   02 PRE-COMPARE-AND-PROCESS-MSG PIC X(120), VALUE
      "  - PERFORMING COMPARE-AND-PROCESS-INPUT-RECS".
   02 PRE-PROCESS-REM-MASTER-MSG  PIC X(120), VALUE
      "  - PERFORMING PROCESS-REMAINING-MASTER-RECS".
   02 PRE-PROCESS-REM-WORK-MSG    PIC X(120), VALUE
      "  - PERFORMING PROCESS-REMAINING-WORK-RECS".
   02 PRE-WARN-EMPTY-PAY-MSG      PIC X(120), VALUE
      "  - PERFORMING WARN-OF-EMPTY-PAY".
   02 PRE-WARN-EMPTY-DECK-MSG     PIC X(120), VALUE
      "  - PERFORMING WARN-OF-EMPTY-DECK".
   02 PRE-PROCESS-PAIR-MSG        PIC X(120), VALUE
      "     - PERFORMING PROCESS-MATCHED-REC-PAIR".
   02 PRE-PROCESS-MASTER-MSG      PIC X(120), VALUE
      "     - PERFORMING PROCESS-UNMATCHED-MASTER-REC".
   02 PRE-PROCESS-WORK-MSG        PIC X(120), VALUE
      "     - PERFORMING PROCESS-UNMATCHED-WORK-REC".
```

```
REPORT SECTION.

   RD BOARD-RPT
           PAGE 66 LINES,  HEADING 4,  FIRST DETAIL 14,
              LAST DETAIL 62.

   01 TYPE REPORT HEADING,  NEXT GROUP NEXT PAGE.
      02 LINE 10.
         03 COLUMN 30,  PIC X(33),
               VALUE  "ATAD COPPER MINE OPERATIONS BOARD".
      02 LINE 15.
         03 COLUMN 16,  PIC X(47),  VALUE
              "SUBJECT: DISLOYAL EMPLOYEES FOR PAYROLL ISSUED".
         03 COLUMN 64,  PIC X(9),   SOURCE IS  TODAYS-DATE
                                     IN  BOARD-RPT-INFO.


   01 TYPE PAGE HEADING.
      02 LINE 4.
         03 COLUMN 59,  PIC X(22), VALUE  "ACM DISLOYAL EMPLOYEES".
      02 LINE 5.
         03 COLUMN 59,  PIC X(9),   SOURCE IS  TODAYS-DATE
                                     IN  BOARD-RPT-INFO.

      02 LINE 6.
         03 COLUMN 59,  PIC X(5),   VALUE  "PAGE:".
         03 COLUMN 65,  PIC Z(3)9,  SOURCE IS  PAGE-COUNTER.
      02 LINE 10.
         03 COLUMN 16,  PIC X(9),   VALUE  "ID NUMBER".
         03 COLUMN 27,  PIC X(4),   VALUE  "NAME".
         03 COLUMN 59,  PIC X(5),   VALUE  "HOURS".
         03 COLUMN 72,  PIC X(4),   VALUE  "BONDS".
      02 LINE 11.
         03 COLUMN 16,  PIC X(9),   VALUE  "---------".
         03 COLUMN 27,  PIC X(4),   VALUE  "----".
         C3 COLUMN 59,  PIC X(5),   VALUE  "-----".
         03 COLUMN 72,  PIC X(4),   VALUE  "----".

   01 DISLOYAL-EMPL-LINE     TYPE DETAIL,  LINE PLUS 1.
      02 COLUMN 16,  PIC 9(9),
           SOURCE IS  ID-NUM IN DISLOYAL-EMPL-LINE-ITEMS.
      02 COLUMN 27,  PIC X(30),
           SOURCE IS  NAME IN DISLOYAL-EMPL-LINE-ITEMS.
      02 COLUMN 59,  PIC Z(2)9.9(2),  SOURCE IS
           TOTAL-HOURS-WORKED IN DISLOYAL-EMPL-LINE-ITEMS.
      02 COLUMN 72,  PIC X(3),  SOURCE IS
           BOND-PURCHASE-INDICATION IN DISLOYAL-EMPL-LINE-ITEMS.

   01 SUMMATION-LINE     TYPE DETAIL,  LINE PLUS 4.
      02 COLUMN 18,  PIC X(35),
           VALUE  "*** NUMBER OF DISLOYAL EMPLOYEES =".
      02 COLUMN 54,  PIC Z(5)9,
           SOURCE IS  NUM-DISLOYAL-EMPL IN BOARD-RPT-INFO.
```

```
PROCEDURE DIVISION.


DECLARATIVES.

VERIFY-LEVEL-1  SECTION.
    USE FOR DEBUGGING ON      WARN-OF-EMPTY-INPUTS,
                              WARN-OF-EMPTY-OLD-MASTER,
                              WARN-OF-EMPTY-WORK,
                              PRODUCE-PAYROLL-AND-RPT.

  ACT-ACCORDINGLY.
    DISPLAY  LOG-HEADER  UPON  VERIFICATION-PRINTER.
    DISPLAY  SPACES  UPON  VERIFICATION-PRINTER.
    DISPLAY  SPACES  UPON  VERIFICATION-PRINTER.

    IF (DEBUG-NAME  = "PRODUCE-PAYROLL-AND-RPT")
          DISPLAY  PRE-PRODUCE-PAYROLL-MSG
              UPON  VERIFICATION-PRINTER
    ELSE IF (DEBUG-NAME  =  "WARN-OF-EMPTY-INPUTS")
          DISPLAY  PRE-WARN-EMPTY-INPUTS-MSG
              UPON  VERIFICATION-PRINTER
    ELSE IF (DEBUG-NAME  =  "WARN-OF-EMPTY-OLD-MASTER")
          DISPLAY  PRE-WARN-EMPTY-MASTER-MSG
              UPON  VERIFICATION-PRINTER
    ELSE IF (DEBUG-NAME  =  "WARN-OF-EMPTY-WORK")
          DISPLAY  PRE-WARN-EMPTY-WORK-MSG
              UPON  VERIFICATION-PRINTER.


VERIFY-LEVEL-2  SECTION.
    USE FOR DEBUGGING ON      COMPARE-AND-PROCESS-INPUT-RECS,
                              PROCESS-REMAINING-MASTER-RECS,
                              PROCESS-REMAINING-WORK-RECS,
                              WARN-OF-EMPTY-PAY,
                              WARN-OF-EMPTY-DECK.

  ACT-ACCORDINGLY.
    IF (DEBUG-NAME  =  "COMPARE-AND-PROCESS-INPUT-RECS")
          DISPLAY  PRE-COMPARE-AND-PROCESS-MSG
              UPON  VERIFICATION-PRINTER
          DISPLAY  "    EMPL-PAYROLL-REC = ",
                   EMPL-PAYROLL-REC IN OLD-PAYROLL-MASTER-FILE
              UPON  VERIFICATION-PRINTER
          DISPLAY  "    EMPL-WORK-REC   = ",  EMPL-WORK-REC
              UPON  VERIFICATION-PRINTER

    ELSE IF (DEBUG-NAME  =  "PROCESS-REMAINING-MASTER-RECS")
          DISPLAY  PRE-PROCESS-REM-MASTER-MSG
              UPON  VERIFICATION-PRINTER
          DISPLAY  "    EMPL-PAYROLL-REC = ",
                   EMPTY-PAYROLL-REC IN OLD-PAYROLL-MASTER-FILE
              UPON  VERIFICATION-PRINTER

    ELSE IF (DEBUG-NAME  =  "PROCESS-REMAINING-WORK-RECS")
          DISPLAY  PRE-PROCESS-REM-WORK-MSG
              UPON  VERIFICATION-PRINTER
          DISPLAY  "    EMPL-WORK-REC = ",  EMPL-WORK-REC
              UPON  VERIFICATION-PRINTER
```

```
          ELSE IF (DEBUG-NAME  =  "WARN-OF-EMPTY-PAY")
                  DISPLAY  PRE-WARN-EMPTY-PAY-MSG
                     UPON  VERIFICATION-PRINTER

          ELSE IF (DEBUG-NAME  =  "WARN-OF-EMPTY-DECK")
                  DISPLAY  PRE-WARN-EMPTY-DECK-MSG
                     UPON  VERIFICATION-PRINTER.


   VERIFY-LEVEL-3  SECTION.
          USE FOR DEBUGGING ON     PROCESS-MATCHED-REC-PAIR,
                                   PROCESS-UNMATCHED-MASTER-REC,
                                   PROCESS-UNMATCHED-WORK-REC.

      ACT-ACCORDINGLY.
          IF (DEBUG-NAME  =  "PROCESS-MATCHED-REC-PAIR")
                  DISPLAY  PRE-PROCESS-PAIR-MSG
                     UPON  VERIFICATION-PRINTER
          ELSE IF (DEBUG-NAME  =  "PROCESS-UNMATCHED-MASTER-REC")
                  DISPLAY  PRE-PROCESS-MASTER-MSG
                     UPON  VERIFICATION-PRINTER
          ELSE IF (DEBUG-NAME  =  "PROCESS-UNMATCHED-WORK-REC")
                  DISPLAY  PRE-PROCESS-WORK-MSG
                     UPON  VERIFICATION-PRINTER.


   VERIFY-LEVEL-4  SECTION.
          USE FOR DEBUGGING ON    NET-PAY-CALC-CONDITION.

      ACT-ACCORDINGLY.
          DISPLAY  "        TOTAL-HOURS-WORKED = ",
                            TOTAL-HOURS-WORKED IN CALC-ITEMS,
                   ",  GROSS-PAY = ",
                            GROSS-PAY IN CALC-ITEMS,
                   ",  STATE-TAX = ",
                            STATE-TAX IN CALC-ITEMS,
                   ",  BOND-DEDUCTION = ",
                            BOND-DEDUCTION IN CALC-ITEMS
             UPON  VERIFICATION-PRINTER.
          DISPLAY  "        NET-PAY = ",  NET-PAY IN CALC-ITEMS,
                   ",  NET-PAY-CALC-CONDITION = ",
                            NET-PAY-CALC-CONDITION IN CALC-ITEMS
             UPON  VERIFICATION-PRINTER.


   END DECLARATIVES.
```

```
LEVEL-1-MODULES  SECTION.

  MAIN-PROGRAM.
    OPEN INPUT    OLD-PAYROLL-MASTER-FILE,  WORK-REC-FILE.
    MOVE ZERO TO  OLD-PAYROLL-MASTER-FILE-STATUS,
                  WORK-REC-FILE-STATUS.

    PERFORM  GET-NEXT-OLD-MASTER-REC.
    PERFORM  GET-NEXT-WORK-REC.

    IF (EOF-OLD-PAYROLL-MASTER-FILE) AND (EOF-WORK-REC-FILE)
            PERFORM  WARN-OF-EMPTY-INPUTS
    ELSE IF (EOF-OLD-PAYROLL-MASTER-FILE)
             AND (NOT  EOF-WORK-REC-FILE)
            PERFORM  WARN-OF-EMPTY-OLD-MASTER
    ELSE IF (NOT  EOF-OLD-PAYROLL-MASTER-FILE)
             AND (EOF-WORK-REC-FILE)
            PERFORM  WARN-OF-EMPTY-WORK
    ELSE IF (NOT  EOF-OLD-PAYROLL-MASTER-FILE)
             AND (NOT  EOF-WORK-REC-FILE)
            PERFORM  PRODUCE-PAYROLL-AND-RPT.

    CLOSE  OLD-PAYROLL-MASTER-FILE,  WORK-REC-FILE.
    STOP RUN.
```

```
LEVEL-2-MODULES  SECTION.

   PRODUCE-PAYROLL-AND-RPT.
       OPEN OUTPUT    PAY-REC-FILE,  OPERATIONS-BOARD-RPT,
                      NEW-PAYROLL-MASTER-FILE,
                      ILLEGAL-WORK-REC-DECK.
       CALL  "GET-ANSI-DATE"
          USING  TODAYS-DATE IN BOARD-RPT-INFO.
       INITIATE  BOARD-RPT.
       MOVE ZERO TO  NUM-DISLOYAL-EMPL,
                     SIZE-PAY-REC-FILE,
                     SIZE-ILLEGAL-WORK-REC-DECK.

       PERFORM  COMPARE-AND-PROCESS-INPUT-RECS
          UNTIL (EOF-OLD-PAYROLL-MASTER-FILE) OR (EOF-WORK-REC-FILE).
       IF (NOT  EOF-OLD-PAYROLL-MASTER-FILE)
          PERFORM  PROCESS-REMAINING-MASTER-RECS
             UNTIL (EOF-OLD-PAYROLL-MASTER-FILE).
       IF (NOT  EOF-WORK-REC-FILE)
          PERFORM  PROCESS-REMAINING-WORK-RECS
             UNTIL (EOF-WORK-REC-FILE).

       GENERATE  SUMMATION-LINE.

       IF (EMPTY-PAY-REC-FILE)
          PERFORM  WARN-OF-EMPTY-PAY.
       IF (EMPTY-ILLEGAL-WORK-REC-DECK)
          PERFORM  WARN-OF-EMPTY-DECK.

       TERMINATE  BOARD-RPT.
       CLOSE  PAY-REC-FILE, OPERATIONS-BOARD-RPT,
              NEW-PAYROLL-MASTER-FILE,  ILLEGAL-WORK-REC-DECK.
```

```
LEVEL-3-MODULES  SECTION.

   COMPARE-AND-PROCESS-INPUT-RECS.
      IF (ID-NUM IN EMPL-PAYROLL-REC IN OLD-PAYROLL-MASTER-FILE
          IS EQUAL TO  ID-NUM IN EMPL-WORK-REC)
          PERFORM  PROCESS-MATCHED-REC-PAIR
          PERFORM  GET-NEXT-OLD-MASTER-REC
          PERFORM  GET-NEXT-WORK-REC

      ELSE IF (ID-NUM IN EMPL-PAYROLL-REC
                              IN OLD-PAYROLL-MASTER-FILE
              IS LESS THAN  ID-NUM IN EMPL-WORK-REC)
          PERFORM  PROCESS-UNMATCHED-MASTER-REC
          PERFORM  GET-NEXT-OLD-MASTER-REC

      ELSE IF (ID-NUM IN EMPL-PAYROLL-REC
                              IN OLD-PAYROLL-MASTER-FILE
              IS GREATER THAN  ID-NUM IN EMPL-WORK-REC)
          PERFORM  PROCESS-UNMATCHED-WORK-REC
          PERFORM  GET-NEXT-WORK-REC.


   PROCESS-REMAINING-MASTER-RECS.
      PERFORM  PROCESS-UNMATCHED-MASTER-REC.
      PERFORM  GET-NEXT-OLD-MASTER-REC.


   PROCESS-REMAINING-WORK-RECS.
      PERFORM  PROCESS-UNMATCHED-WORK-REC.
      PERFORM  GET-NEXT-WORK-REC.
```

```
LEVEL-4-MODULES SECTION.

   PROCESS-MATCHED-REC-PAIR.
      COMPUTE  TOTAL-HOURS-WORKED IN CALC-ITEMS   =
                       STRAIGHT-TIME-HOURS IN EMPL-WORK-REC  +
                       OVERTIME-HOURS IN EMPL-WORK-REC.
      IF (TOTAL-HOURS-WORKED IN CALC-ITEMS  = 0)
         MOVE  ZERO-TOTAL-HOURS-MSG
               TO  REASON-WORK-REC-ILLEGAL
         PERFORM  PRODUCE-ILLEGAL-WORK-REC-CARD
         ADD 1 TO  SIZE-ILLEGAL-WORK-REC-DECK
         PERFORM  PROCESS-UNMATCHED-MASTER-REC
      ELSE
         PERFORM  CALC-GROSS-PAY
         PERFORM  CALC-STATE-TAX
         PERFORM  CALC-BOND-DEDUCTION
         PERFORM  CALC-NET-PAY
         IF (BOND-NOT-AFFORDABLE)
            MOVE  CANT-AFFORD-BOND-MSG
                  TO  REASON-WORK-REC-ILLEGAL
            PERFORM  PRODUCE-ILLEGAL-WORK-REC-CARD
            ADD 1 TO  SIZE-ILLEGAL-WORK-REC-DECK
            PERFORM  PROCESS-UNMATCHED-MASTER-REC
         ELSE
            PERFORM  PRODUCE-EMPL-PAY-REC
            ADD 1 TO  SIZE-PAY-REC-FILE
            PERFORM  PRODUCE-UPDATED-NEW-MASTER-REC
            IF (TOTAL-HOURS-WORKED IN CALC-ITEMS
                        IS LESS THAN   EXPECTED-MINIMUM-HOURS)
               OR (EMPL-WANTS-NO-BOND)
             PERFORM  PRODUCE-DISLOYAL-EMPL-LINE
             ADD 1 TO  NUM-DISLOYAL-EMPL.


   PROCESS-UNMATCHED-MASTER-REC.
      MOVE CORRESPONDING  EMPL-PAYROLL-REC
                          IN OLD-PAYROLL-MASTER-FILE
         TO  DISLOYAL-EMPL-LINE-ITEMS.
      MOVE ZERO TO  TOTAL-HOURS-WORKED IN DISLOYAL-EMPL-LINE-ITEMS.
      MOVE  NO-BOND-BOUGHT-INDICATION
         TO  BOND-PURCHASE-INDICATION IN DISLOYAL-EMPL-LINE-ITEMS.
      GENERATE  DISLOYAL-EMPL-LINE.
      ADD 1 TO  NUM-DISLOYAL-EMPL.
      PERFORM  COPY-OLD-MASTER-REC-AS-NEW.


   PROCESS-UNMATCHED-WORK-REC.
      MOVE  UNMATCHED-MSG  TO  REASON-WORK-REC-ILLEGAL.
      PERFORM  PRODUCE-ILLEGAL-WORK-REC-CARD.
      ADD 1 TO  SIZE-ILLEGAL-WORK-REC-DECK.
```

```
LEVEL-5-MODULES  SECTION.

  CALC-GROSS-PAY.
    COMPUTE  STRAIGHT-TIME-PAY  ROUNDED  =

              (STRAIGHT-TIME-HOURS IN EMPL-WORK-REC) *
                 (HOURLY-WAGE IN EMPL-PAYROLL-REC
                               IN OLD-PAYROLL-MASTER-FILE).

    COMPUTE  OVERTIME-PAY  ROUNDED  =

              (OVERTIME-HOURS IN EMPL-WORK-REC) * OVERTIME-FACTOR *
                 (HOURLY-WAGE IN EMPL-PAYROLL-REC
                               IN OLD-PAYROLL-MASTER-FILE).

    COMPUTE  GROSS-PAY  =  STRAIGHT-TIME-PAY  +  OVERTIME-PAY.


  CALC-STATE-TAX.
    COMPUTE  STATE-TAX  ROUNDED  =
                    (STATE-TAX-RATE * GROSS-PAY)
                  (FAMILY-SIZE IN EMPL-PAYROLL-REC
                               IN OLD-PAYROLL-MASTER-FILE).


  CALC-BOND-DEDUCTION.
    IF (EMPL-WANTS-BOND)
      MOVE  STD-BOND-DEDUCTION  TO  BOND-DEDUCTION
    ELSE
      MOVE ZERO TO  BOND-DEDUCTION.


  CALC-NET-PAY.
    COMPUTE  BEFORE-BOND-PAY  =  GROSS-PAY  -  STATE-TAX.
    IF (BEFORE-BOND-PAY  <  BOND-DEDUCTION)
      MOVE ZERO TO  NET-PAY IN CALC-ITEMS
      MOVE 1 TO  NET-PAY-CALC-CONDITION
    ELSE
      COMPUTE  NET-PAY IN CALC-ITEMS  =
                       BEFORE-BOND-PAY - BOND-DEDUCTION
      MOVE ZERO TO  NET-PAY-CALC-CONDITION.
```

```
OLD-PAYROLL-MASTER-I-O  SECTION.

  GET-NEXT-OLD-MASTER-REC.
    READ  OLD-PAYROLL-MASTER-FILE
    AT END    MOVE 1 TO  OLD-PAYROLL-MASTER-FILE-STATUS.


WORK-REC-FILE-I-O  SECTION.

  GET-NEXT-WORK-REC.
    READ  WORK-REC-FILE
    AT END    MOVE 1 TO  WORK-REC-FILE-STATUS.


PAY-REC-FILE-I-O  SECTION.

  PRODUCE-EMPL-PAY-REC.
    MOVE  CORRESPONDING  EMPL-PAYROLL-REC
                                IN OLD-PAYROLL-MASTER-FILE
          TO  EMPL-PAY-REC.
    MOVE  NET-PAY IN CALC-ITEMS
          TO NET-PAY IN EMPL-PAY-REC.
    WRITE  EMPL-PAY-REC.


NEW-PAYROLL-MASTER-I-O  SECTION.

  COPY-OLD-MASTER-REC-AS-NEW.
    MOVE  EMPL-PAYROLL-REC IN OLD-PAYROLL-MASTER-FILE
          TO  EMPL-PAYROLL-REC IN NEW-PAYROLL-MASTER-FILE.
    PERFORM  FREE-NEW-MASTER-REC.

  PRODUCE-UPDATED-NEW-MASTER-REC.
    MOVE  EMPL-PAYROLL-REC IN OLD-PAYROLL-MASTER-FILE
          TO  EMPL-PAYROLL-REC IN NEW-PAYROLL-MASTER-FILE.
    ADD  GROSS-PAY IN CALC-ITEMS
          TO  YEAR-TO-DATE-GROSS-PAY IN EMPL-PAYROLL-REC
                  IN NEW-PAYROLL-MASTER-FILE.
    ADD  STATE-TAX IN CALC-ITEMS
      TO  YEAR-TO-DATE-TAXES IN EMPL-PAYROLL-REC
                  IN NEW-PAYROLL-MASTER-FILE.
    PERFORM  FREE-NEW-MASTER-REC.

  FREE-NEW-MASTER-REC.
    WRITE  EMPL-PAYROLL-REC IN NEW-PAYROLL-MASTER-FILE.
```

```
OPERATIONS-BOARD-RPT-I-O  SECTION.

   PRODUCE-DISLOYAL-EMPL-LINE.
      MOVE CORRESPONDING  EMPL-PAYROLL-REC
                            IN OLD-PAYROLL-MASTER-FILE
            TO DISLOYAL-EMPL-LINE-ITEMS.
      MOVE  TOTAL-HOURS-WORKED IN CALC-ITEMS
            TO  TOTAL-HOURS-WORKED IN DISLOYAL-EMPL-LINE-ITEMS.
      IF (EMPL-WANTS-BOND)
         MOVE  BOND-BOUGHT-INDICATION IN BOARD-RPT-INFO
               TO  BOND-PURCHASE-INDICATION
                            IN DISLOYAL-EMPL-LINE-ITEMS
      ELSE
         MOVE  NO-BOND-BOUGHT-INDICATION IN BOARD-RPT-INFO
               TO  BOND-PURCHASE-INDICATION
                            IN DISLOYAL-EMPL-LINE-ITEMS.

      GENERATE  DISLOYAL-EMPL-LINE.


ILLEGAL-WORK-REC-DECK-I-O  SECTION.

   PRODUCE-ILLEGAL-WORK-REC-CARD.
      MOVE SPACES TO  ILLEGAL-WORK-REC-CARD.
      MOVE CORRESPONDING  EMPL-WORK-REC
            TO  ILLEGAL-WORK-REC-CARD.
      MOVE  REASON-WORK-REC-ILLEGAL
            TO  REASON-ILLEGAL IN ILLEGAL-WORK-REC-CARD.
      WRITE  ILLEGAL-WORK-REC-CARD.
```

```
SYSTEM-OPERATOR-I-O   SECTION.

   WARN-OF-EMPTY-INPUTS.
      MOVE SPACES TO  PROGRAM-MSG.
         PERFORM  PRINT-PROGRAM-MSG.
      MOVE  INTRO-MSG  TO  PROGRAM-MSG.
         PERFORM  PRINT-PROGRAM-MSG.
      MOVE  EMPTY-INPUTS-MSG  TO  PROGRAM-MSG.
         PERFORM  PRINT-PROGRAM-MSG.
      MOVE  ABORT-MSG  TO  PROGRAM-MSG.
         PERFORM  PRINT-PROGRAM-MSG.

   WARN-OF-EMPTY-OLD-MASTER.
      MOVE SPACES TO  PROGRAM-MSG.
         PERFORM  PRINT-PROGRAM-MSG.
      MOVE  INTRO-MSG  TO  PROGRAM-MSG.
         PERFORM  PRINT-PROGRAM-MSG.
      MOVE  EMPTY-OLD-MASTER-MSG  TO  PROGRAM-MSG.
         PERFORM  PRINT-PROGRAM-MSG.
      MOVE  ABORT-MSG  TO  PROGRAM-MSG.
         PERFORM  PRINT-PROGRAM-MSG.

   WARN-OF-EMPTY-WORK.
      MOVE SPACES TO  PROGRAM-MSG.
         PERFORM  PRINT-PROGRAM-MSG.
      MOVE  INTRO-MSG  TO  PROGRAM-MSG.
         PERFORM  PRINT-PROGRAM-MSG.
      MOVE  EMPTY-WORK-MSG  TO  PROGRAM-MSG.
         PERFORM  PRINT-PROGRAM-MSG.
      MOVE  ABORT-MSG  TO  PROGRAM-MSG.
         PERFORM  PRINT-PROGRAM-MSG.

   WARN-OF-EMPTY-PAY.
      MOVE SPACES TO  PROGRAM-MSG.
         PERFORM  PRINT-PROGRAM-MSG.
      MOVE  INTRO-MSG  TO  PROGRAM-MSG.
         PERFORM  PRINT-PROGRAM-MSG.
      MOVE  NO-LEGAL-WORK-RECS-MSG  TO  PROGRAM-MSG.
         PERFORM  PRINT-PROGRAM-MSG.
      MOVE  EMPTY-PAY-MSG  TO  PROGRAM-MSG.
         PERFORM  PRINT-PROGRAM-MSG.

   WARN-OF-EMPTY-DECK.
      MOVE SPACES TO  PROGRAM-MSG.
         PERFORM  PRINT-PROGRAM-MSG.
      MOVE  INTRO-MSG  TO  PROGRAM-MSG.
         PERFORM  PRINT-PROGRAM-MSG.
      MOVE  ALL-LEGAL-WORK-RECS-MSG  TO  PROGRAM-MSG.
         PERFORM  PRINT-PROGRAM-MSG.
      MOVE  EMPTY-ILLEGAL-DECK-MSG  TO  PROGRAM-MSG.
         PERFORM  PRINT-PROGRAM-MSG.

   PRINT-PROGRAM-MSG.
      DISPLAY  PROGRAM-MSG.
```

Example 3.2   Three COBOL Library Texts Copied into the Payroll and Report Program

```
(1)      FD PAYROLL-MASTER-FILE
            BLOCK CONTAINS 10 RECORDS,
            LABEL RECORDS STANDARD,
            VALUE OF ID IS  "ACM PAYROLL MASTER".
         01 EMPL-PAYROLL-REC.
            02 ID-NUM                    PIC   9(9).
            02 NAME                      PIC   X(30).
            02 HOURLY-WAGE               PIC   9V9(2).
            02 FAMILY-SIZE               PIC   9(2).
            02 YEAR-TO-DATE-GROSS-PAY    PIC   9(6)V9(2).
            02 YEAR-TO-DATE-TAXES        PIC   9(5)V9(2).


(2)      FD WORK-REC-FILE
            BLOCK CONTAINS 10 RECORDS,
            LABEL RECORDS STANDARD,
            VALUE OF ID IS  "ACM WEEKLY WORK RECORDS".
         01 EMPL-WORK-REC.
            02 ID-NUM                    PIC   9(9).
            02 STRAIGHT-TIME-HOURS       PIC   9(2)V9(2).
            02 OVERTIME-HOURS            PIC   9(2)V9(2).
            02 BOND-OPTION-INDICATION    PIC   X(1).
               88 EMPL-WANTS-BOND           VALUE  "Y".
               88 EMPL-WANTS-NO-BOND        VALUE  "N".


(3)      FD PAY-REC-FILE
            BLOCK CONTAINS 10 RECORDS,
            LABEL RECORDS STANDARD,
            VALUE OF ID IS  "ACM PAY RECORDS".
         01 EMPL-PAY-REC.
            02 ID-NUM    PIC   9(9).
            02 NAME      PIC   X(30).
            02 NET-PAY   PIC   9(4)V9(2).
```

EXERCISES

Exercise 3.1 (Think First, Code Later)
Would it have been more practical for Mr. Coleman to recommend to General Roht that he spend a few bucks to buy the payroll and report program used by the International Data Processing Company rather than develop a replacement?

Exercise 3.2 (Programming Proverbs)
List three ways in which Irene and Dorothy followed the proverb, "Plan for Change."

Exercise 3.3 (Programming Approaches)
Write a short position paper comparing the "top-down" approach with the "systems analyst" approach in Proverb 6 of Chapter 2.

Exercise 3.4 (Detailing Inputs and Outputs)
How should Figure 3.4 be modified if the tape label consists of three components instead of merely one? More generally, exactly what needs to be detailed in order to specify a tape input or output? Develop a reasonable format for presenting needed detail.

Exercise 3.5 (The Input/Output Mapping)
Is there any way of grouping the system operator messages that occur in various places under condition 2.4 of the condition-action list of Figure 3.9?

Exercise 3.6 (The Input/Output Mapping)
Develop an alternative to the condition-action list method for expressing how a program is to map input situations to output responses. Consider a decision table approach.

Exercise 3.7 (Implementation Requirements)
A typical requirement for a program being implemented is that it occupy no more than a certain amount of fast memory. To meet this requirement, a programmer has to be very careful in choosing the overall algorithm and, at a lower level, has to consider the use of the SAME AREA clause of the Environment Division. Give two other concerns that could be important implementation considerations on particular programming projects. For each concern outline a number of ways of dealing with it.

Exercise 3.8 (Program Levels)
Draw a complete tree in the form of Figure 3.2 to illustrate the levels of the final payroll and report program.

Exercise 3.9   (Writing the Levels of a Given Program)
Write a sequence of levels that might have been used to generate the
program of Example 2.6b in the prettyprint proverb of Chapter 2.

Exercise 3.10   (Program Modifications)
Suppose that the operations board now wishes to have statistics stating the
total gross payroll, total tax paid, the total bond purchase, total net
payroll, and the average hours worked per employee. Assign someone to
act as the head of the operations board. Modify the payroll and report
program to print the desired statistics.

Exercise 3.11   (Program Modifications)
Modify the payroll and report program to accept input tapes identified
also by a date of generation. Ensure that the payroll and report program
processes only input tapes dated no more than six days previously. The
program should also label the output tapes with the current date. A date is
coded as with the ACCEPT verb.

Exercise 3.12   (Program Modifications)
Dorothy built in verification aids for the payroll and report program in
Example 3.1. The aids proved very valuable for initial testing. However,
once testing progressed to rather large input files, the verification aids
dumped too much information. How would you change the aids for
testing with large input files? Must you actually remove the aids that are
inappropriate for such tests?

Exercise 3.13   (Program Development)
Write an informal and formal statement of the P_3 module "process
matched record pair" for the payroll and report program.

Exercise 3.14   (Program Development)
Assume you need a program that lists a COBOL source program. In listing,
you want the option of being able to blank out the sequence number area
and the program identification area, and to omit debugging lines. Develop
this program top-down, documenting each step.

Exercise 3.15   (Program Development)
Following the same specification and top-down development strategy as
Irene, present a complete program to solve the following problem:

 Input: A sequence of characters representing the text of a letter. The
            text contains only alphabetic English words, blanks, commas,
            periods, and the special word "PP" denoting the beginning
            of a paragraph.

Output: 1. The number of words in the text
2. The text given as input, printed according to the following format:

    a. The first line of each paragraph is to be indented five spaces and successive lines are to be left-adjusted. Lines are printed in units of 60 or fewer characters.

    b. One blank is to separate each word from the previous word, comma, or period.

    c. A word cannot be broken across lines.

Exercise 3.16 (Programming Pressure)
Will Irene take over Mr. Coleman's job?

CHAPTER FOUR
PROGRAM STANDARDS

"Any programmer who fails to comply with the standard naming, formatting or commenting conventions should be shot. If it so happens that it is inconvenient to shoot him, then he is to be politely requested to recode his program in adherence to the above standard."

Michael Spier [Ref. S1]

The COBOL language has been with us since 1960, yet the writing of high-quality COBOL programs has remained a matter of personal style. The thrust of this chapter is to go beyond the "proverbs" and present some rigorous standards for the writing of COBOL programs. Developing rigorous program standards is not easy, for the rules must be unambiguous, of sufficient merit so that a programmer will not be unduly stifled by their adoption, and ideally, machine testable. We have followed this chapter's program standards throughout this book.

The importance of developing such standards is clear. For both managers and programmers, there is a need to develop uniform rules so that more programmers may more easily understand programs, a need to develop coding techniques that reduce the complexity of programs, and a need to control the entire software development effort.

Program standards are part of a much larger effort to promote the writing of quality COBOL programs. That effort includes an expansion of the work presented here [Ref. L4] and a methodology for writing very large programs [Refs. C1 and C2].

No attempt is made here to encompass every feature of the COBOL language. No standard can attempt to cover every aspect of a given programming problem. Nevertheless, the standards presented in this book should go a long way to promote quality programs. Furthermore, no attempt is made to consider the consequences if the adoption of standards results in the loss of efficiency. Too great a loss may be due cause for revocation of some standards.

GENERAL RULES

[GEN-1]   *Any violation of the program standards must be approved by the project management.*

The rationale here is to allow exceptions to the program standards, but only if management approves. It is critical that all program standards, unless waived, be followed to the very last detail.

[GEN-2]   *For the installation and for each application there must be a standard set of user-defined words chosen before coding.*

The following set of words is a sample of those that might be adopted for an inventory problem:

PAGE-NUM	For generating page numbers
LINE-NUM	For counting lines
TRANSACTION-REC	For input to a fine updating program
QTY-IN-STOCK	For quantities on hand
CUST-ACCT-NUM	For customer account numbers
UNIT-COST	For the cost of single items
INVENTORY-FILE	For inventory files
DATE-PURCHASED	For dates of purchase
FLOOR-NUM	For floor numbers
PART-NUM	For part numbers

The rationale here is to develop a well-accepted set of naming conventions and to reduce the time spent by programmers in devising good mnemonic words. This rule promotes readability of programs and prevents confusion caused by having different names for the same objects. Enforcement of the standard names is best accomplished through the use of a library of COBOL Data Division entries and Procedure Division procedures. These can be inserted in programs using the COPY verb.

[GEN-3]   *The logical parts of a user-defined word must be separated by hyphens.*

For example, use

NET-PAY		NETPAY
X-OUTPUT-REC	not	XOUTPUT-REC
CUST-ACCT-NUM		CUST-ACCTNUM

The rationale here is to promote the use of readable names.

[GEN-4]   *Every installation must establish prettyprinting conventions.*

The rationale here is to promote readability and to save time by developing a fixed set of rules once and for all. See the Appendix for the prettyprinting standards used in this book.

IDENTIFICATION DIVISION RULES

[ID-1]   *The AUTHOR paragraph in every program not for public use must include (1) the name of the group(s) responsible for the program, (2) the name of the project director, and (3) the names of everyone who has helped to write or change the code.*

The rationale here is to allow quicker access to the originators of a program if problems should arise during program development.

[ID-2]   *The Identification Division must be followed by comment lines that give a brief description of the program's intent, required inputs, expected outputs, and a reference to the relevant external documents.*

The rationale here is to give a synopsis of the program to all readers.

[ID-3]   *After a program is in public use, comment lines describing a modification must be added before every recompilation.*

The comment lines must give the following:

1. An index <MOD-01>, <MOD-02>, . . . , of the current modification
2. The change from the previous compilation
3. The reason for the change
4. The person making the change, and the date.

For example, use

```
*  <MOD-01>  "INVALID KEY" PHRASE ADDED TO THE READ
*                     STATEMENT IN GET-NEXT-MASTER-REC.
*             REASON: INPUT VALIDATION MISSES ILLEGAL
*                     TRANSACTION PART NUMBERS.
*             75 AUG 08,     E. J. CARTER
```

If equivalent external facilities exist, these comment lines may be omitted. The rationale here is to make error detection in operational programs easier. As is often the case, a change made to a program may introduce errors in other program sections. The modification record can be an invaluable aid in detecting such errors.

DATA DIVISION RULES

[DATA-1]   *For all data description entries immediately subordinate to a 01 entry, the level number 02 is to be used. For entries immediately subordinate to level 02 entry, the level number 03 is to be used, and so forth.*

For example, use the schema at the left rather than at the right:

01 INVENTORY-REC.	01 INVENTORY-REC.
02 PART-NUM	10 PART-NUM
02 LOCATION	10 LOCATION
03 STATE	22 STATE
03 WAREHOUSE	22 WAREHOUSE
04 FLOOR-NUM	33 FLOOR-NUM
04 BIN	33 BIN
02 QTY-IN-STOCK	10 QTY-IN-STOCK
02 UNIT-COST	10 UNIT-COST
02 DATE-PURCHASED	10 DATE-PURCHASED
03 YEAR	12 YEAR
03 MONTH	12 MONTH

The rationale here is to make the level numbers identical to the logical levels of the structure. Even the convenience of successive level numbers such as 01, 05, 10, 15 to allow for easy insertions when changes are required in the record structure does not outweigh the clarity of the 01, 02, 03 rule.

[DATA-2]   *Except when performing editing, PICTURE clause character strings must not contain sequences of two or more identical symbols.*

For example, use the string at the left rather than at the right:

02 FILLER PICTURE X(4).	02 FILLER PICTURE XXXX.
02 DEPT-NUM PICTURE 9(6).	02 DEPT-NUM PICTURE 999999.
02 PRICE PICTURE 9(4)V9(2).	02 PRICE PICTURE 9999V99.

The rationale here is to eliminate the need for counting possibly lengthy sequences of picture characters and to highlight possible data alignment problems occurring on data movement.

[DATA-3]   *No 77 entries are allowed in the WORKING-STORAGE section.*

For example, use

```
01  GLOBAL-COUNTERS.
    02  PAGE-NUM       PICTURE 9(2).
    02  LINE-NUM       PICTURE 9(2).
    02  RECORD-NUM     PICTURE 9(4).
```

rather than a list of 77 level entries. The rationale here is to require structuring of related data items under level 01 entries.

[DATA-4]   *All specifications of permanent input and output files used by a program must be described in a COBOL library.*

The rationale here is to place specifications of commonly used files in a common library so that all programs that access the files can simply copy the correct specifications and maintain uniform naming conventions.

[DATA-5]   *All data items that remain constant throughout a program must be initialized in a VALUE clause. No statement may change the value of a constant data item.*

For example,

```
02  NUM-MENS-SUIT-STYLES    PICTURE 9(3),  VALUE 103.
...
ADD 1 TO  NUM-MENS-SUIT-STYLES.
```

is not allowed. The rationale here is to make constants visible in the Data Division where they can be easily found and, if need be, *changed.*

[DATA-6]   *All message literals printed by a COBOL program must be specified in the VALUE clause of a data description entry that has a mnemonic data name.*

For example, use

```
02  EXCESS-DEDUCTIONS-MSG  PIC  X(50),
        VALUE  "EMPLOYEE DEDUCTIONS EXCEEDED GROSS-PAY.".
...
MOVE  EXCESS-DEDUCTIONS-MSG  TO  PAY-CALC-ERROR-MSG.
```

not

MOVE "EMPLOYEE DEDUCTIONS EXCEEDED GROSS-PAY."
    TO PAY-CALC-ERROR-MSG.

The rationale here is to acknowledge the fact that program messages are program constants.

PROCEDURE DIVISION RULES

[PROC-1]   *Input-output operations must be isolated in distinct procedures.*

This rule is enforced by allowing only one READ statement per file, requiring distinct procedures that construct and output distinct outputs, and allowing one WRITE statement per file. Extra WRITE statements per file to control page advances are allowable.

For example, use

```
PROCESS-NEXT-TRANSACTION.
    PERFORM  GET-NEXT-TRANSACTION.
    IF  (EOF-TRANSACTION-FILE)
            NEXT SENTENCE
    ELSE
    . . .
GET-NEXT-TRANSACTION.
    READ  TRANSACTION-FILE
        AT END  MOVE 1 TO TRANSACTION-FILE-STATUS.
    IF  (NOT  EOF-TRANSACTION-FILE)
        IF  (TRANSACTION-REC = EOF-MARKER-REC)
            MOVE 1 TO TRANSACTION-FILE-STATUS.
```

not

```
PROCESS-NEXT-TRANSACTION.
    READ  TRANSACTION-FILE
        AT END  MOVE 1 TO  TRANSACTION-FILE-STATUS.
    IF  (NOT  EOF-TRANSACTION-FILE)
        IF  (TRANSACTION-REC  NOT EQUAL  EOF-MARKER-REC)
    . . .
```

The rationale here is to isolate those portions of a program that interface with users and external files.

[PROC-2]   *If there is a reasonable possibility that the type or value of an input data item is not correct, and thus can cause an error in subsequent processing, the type and value of the data item must be validated immediately.*

The rationale here is to make sure that potential errors are detected as soon as possible.

[PROC-3]   *The values of loop control variables associated with the VARY-ING and BY phrases of a PERFORM statement may not be modified within the performed procedure.*

The rationale here is to prevent tricky loop controls.

[PROC-4]   *The maximum length of a paragraph is one page.*

The rationale here is to limit the complexity of a procedure.

[PROC-5]   *GO TO statements are not allowed.*

The rationale here is to force programmers to think ahead and use *only* 1-in, 1-out structures. In COBOL, this means using the IF and PERFORM statements for flow of control. (An exception to the rule is allowed for COBOL implementations that do not have the PERFORM UNTIL construct.) Many programmers at first believe that this standard is unreasonable. With a little practice, however, programming without GO TO's becomes quite easy. When you think you need a GO TO, consider one of the following alternatives:

1. Restructuring the algorithm
2. Performing blocks of code
3. Copying in a piece of code
4. Repeating a condition previously tested
5. Reversing a condition to its negative.

A detailed discussion of this issue will be found in Reference L3.

[PROC-6]   *The THRU option for PERFORM statements is not allowed.*

The rationale here is to make the program logic independent of the physical placement of paragraphs.

[PROC-7]   *Nesting of IF statements may be at most three levels deep.*

If deeper nesting is desired, then procedures should be used. However, the IF verb may be used for a "select-first" or "case" statement of the form,

```
        IF   condition-1
                 statement-1
        ELSE IF   condition-2
                 statement-2
        . . .

        ELSE IF   condition-n
                 statement-n
```

The statements within the case construct may not include IF statements. The rationale here is to avoid confusing conditional constructs.

[PROC-8]   *STOP RUN may only occur as the last statement of the main procedure of a program. EXIT PROGRAM may only occur as the last paragraph of the main procedure of a subprogram.*

The rationale here is to make the logical exit of a program identical to the lexical end of its main procedure.

[PROC-9]   *Arithmetic computations are to be accomplished using the COMPUTE verb.*

There are two exceptions:

1. The ADD and SUBTRACT verbs may be used in the following formats:

$$\text{ADD} \quad \begin{Bmatrix} \text{identifier} \\ \text{literal} \end{Bmatrix} \quad \text{TO} \quad \text{identifier}$$

$$\text{SUBTRACT} \begin{Bmatrix} \text{identifier} \\ \text{literal} \end{Bmatrix} \quad \text{FROM} \quad \text{identifier}$$

2. The DIVIDE verb may be used to compute remainders. For example, use the following:

```
COMPUTE TOTAL-HOURS       = OVERTIME-HOURS + REGULAR-HOURS.
COMPUTE NUM-ON-PAYROLL    = NUM-EMPLOYEES
                              - NUM-ON-VACATION
                              - NUM-ON-LEAVE.
COMPUTE GROSS-PAY         = TOTAL-HOURS * WAGE.
COMPUTE AVG-HOURS         = TOTAL-HOURS / NUM-ON-PAYROLL.
```

not

```
        ADD   OVERTIME-HOURS  TO  REGULAR-HOURS
            GIVING  TOTAL-HOURS.
        SUBTRACT  NUM-ON-VACATION, NUM-ON-LEAVE
            FROM  NUM-EMPLOYEES
            GIVING  NUM-ON-PAYROLL.
        MULTIPLY  TOTAL-HOURS  BY  WAGE
            GIVING  GROSS-PAY.
        DIVIDE  NUM-ON-PAYROLL  INTO  TOTAL-HOURS
            GIVING  AVG-HOURS.
```

The rationale here is to use familiar arithmetic format and operations rather than a somewhat artificial verbal construction. Exception 1 allows a short form for the adding or subtracting of increments. Exception 2 allows computation of remainders, which is not possible with the COMPUTE statement.

[PROC-10]   *Parentheses must be used to specify the order of evaluation for the individual conditions of a complex conditional expression.*

   For example, use the following:

1. IF   (NOT   LEGAL-USER-RESPONSE) AND SHORT-MSG-OPTION-ON
           MOVE   ILLEGAL-INPUT-SHORT-MSG
                  TO   TTY-DISPLAY-LINE
           PERFORM   PRINT-TTY-DISPLAY-LINE.
2. IF   (NOT   LEGAL-SHIFT-NUM)
           OR   ((REGULAR-HRS = 0) AND (OVERTIME-HRS = 0))
           MOVE 2 TO   WORK-REC-CONDITION.

not

1. IF   NOT   LEGAL-USER-RESPONSE   AND   SHORT-MSG-OPTION-ON
           MOVE   ILLEGAL-INPUT-SHORT-MSG
                  TO   TTY-DISPLAY-LINE
           PERFORM   PRINT-TTY-DISPLAY-LINE.
2. IF   NOT   LEGAL-SHIFT-NUM
           OR   REGULAR-HRS = 0   AND   OVERTIME-HRS = 0
           MOVE 2 TO   WORK-REC-CONDITION.

The rationale here is to make logical operations more visible by not relying on the often confusing COBOL condition evaluation rules.

EXERCISES

Exercise 4.1
   Just before press time, we deleted a standard requiring that statements be termined with periods whenever possible, and when not possible, with semicolons. For example:

PERFORM VALIDATE-CARD.
IF (NOT   LEGAL-CARD-REC)
      MOVE 1 TO   CARD-ERROR-DECK-CONDITION;
      PERFORM   PRODUCE-CARD-ERROR-REC;

ELSE
    PERFORM   PRODUCE-DISK-REC-COPY;
    ADD 1 TO   SIZE-DISK-FILE;
    MOVE   ID-NUM IN SALESPERSON-CARD   TO
       ID-NUM-CARD-LAST-COPIED.

What is the major reason for rejecting this standard? Should part of it have been kept?

Exercise 4.2

Many programmers have objected to program standard [DATA-1], suggesting instead that record description level numbers follow the 01, 05, 10, 15 numbering rule, not the 01, 02, 03, 04 rule. Argue your side of this issue.

Exercise 4.3

The following standard was considered for adoption and was ultimately rejected. Can you figure out why?

"The figurative constants,

ZERO, SPACE, HIGH-VALUE, LOW-VALUE

are required only when one character is referenced. Otherwise the constants,

ZEROS, SPACES, HIGH-VALUES, LOW-VALUES

are to be used."

Exercise 4.4

Consider the standard,

"Numbers beginning with decimal points are not allowed."

Can you think of a fraction that violates this standard and yet is clearer than the corresponding fraction with a leading zero attached?

Exercise 4.5

For a long time, we used the following program standard:

"To delineate the body of a PERFORMed procedure, terminate the procedure by an 'empty' paragraph that has the name of the procedure prefixed by the string 'END-'."

For example, we wrote

    VALIDATE-SALESPERSON-CARD.
      MOVE SPACES TO   CARD-ERROR-LIST.

INSPECT   ID-NUM IN SALESPERSON-CARD
   . . .
MOVE "*" TO   CARD-ERROR(5).
END-VALIDATE-SALESPERSON-CARD.

This standard evoked so much controversy that we dropped it. What is your opinion on this use of an empty paragraph?

Exercise 4.6

Pick the program standard you disagree with most and make a case for revoking the standard.

Exercise 4.7

Did we omit a standard that you consider important? Develop the standard, make a case for its adoption, and send us your write-up.

CHAPTER FIVE

ODDS AND ENDS

"Progress is our most important product."
Advertising Slogan of General Electric Corporation

SELECTING MNEMONIC WORDS

When writing COBOL programs it is very tempting to use short and often uninformative user-defined words. The temptation arises because of the extra effort required to devise and actually code more illuminating (usually longer) words. Nevertheless, the choice of user-defined words has a psychological impact that cannot be ignored. Consider the two simple procedures in Example 5.1. Example 5.1b, while longer than Example 5.1a, is a more lucid procedure for calculating gross pay, mainly because of the use of words that are common to payroll calculations.

Good mnemonic user-defined words are a powerful tool for clear documentation, easy verification, and ready maintenance. COBOL has an excellent capability for constructing user-defined words by allowing as many as 30 appropriate characters. We offer four basic principles for devising good user-defined words:

1. Use the standard words established by your customer or programming group.
2. Choose a word that activates the correct "psychological set" [Ref. W1].
3. Avoid words that are not "psychologically distant" [Ref. W1].
4. Be sure to follow consistent naming conventions, and avoid words that can be confused with a system name or a COBOL reserved word.

113

Example 5.1   Using Good Mnemonic Words

```
EXAMPLE 5.1A   POOR


      CALC-GRSS.
      IF (HOURS > NORM)
         COMPUTE  GROSS ROUNDED  =  (NORM * RATE) +
                                    ((HOURS - NORM) * RATE * FACTOR)

      ELSE
         COMPUTE  GROSS ROUNDED  =  HOURS * RATE.




EXAMPLE 5.1B   BETTER


      CALC-GROSS-PAY.
      IF (HOURS-WORKED > STANDARD-WORK-WEEK)
         COMPUTE  STRAIGHT-TIME-PAY  ROUNDED  =
                                 STANDARD-WORK-WEEK * HOURLY-WAGE
         COMPUTE  OVERTIME-HOURS  =
                                 HOURS-WORKED - STANDARD-WORK-WEEK
         COMPUTE  OVERTIME-PAY  ROUNDED  =  OVERTIME-HOURS *
                                 HOURLY-WAGE * OVERTIME-FACTOR
         COMPUTE  GROSS-PAY  ROUNDED  =
                                 STRAIGHT-TIME-PAY + OVERTIME-PAY

      ELSE
         COMPUTE  GROSS-PAY  ROUNDED  =  HOURS-WORKED * HOURLY-WAGE.
```

Standard Words

We encourage the adoption of a full set of standard words for every major programming application. A formal set of standard words makes the selection of good words easy. If your customer or programming manager wants an input record to have the name, MASTER-REC, or a certain field to have the name ORDER-POINT, then these are the "best" words to use, for they make a program consistent with established conventions.

If no formal set of standard words exist, informal standard words and abbreviations are often available. For example, if your customer or group has no special word for an inventory update card deck, an informal standard file name is TRANSACTION-FILE. In the case of a banking-type problem, words like PRIOR-BALANCE, DEPOSITS, WITHDRAWALS, or SERVICE-CHARGE are illuminating informal standards. Furthermore, COBOL programmers have their own familiar conventions. Examples are the following:

TAX-TABLE
REGRESSION-TABLE-INDEX
BOARD-RPT-MAIN-HEADER
CUSTOMER-ID-NUM

OLD-MASTER-REC
NEW-MASTER-REC

The use of words such as these makes a program consistent with informal conventions.

Psychological Set

In psychology the term "psychological set" means a readiness to respond in a specific way to certain stimuli. In the programming context, a "psychological set" means a readiness to associate particular entities or properties with a word. Entities such as social security number, rates of pay, and people's names have many possible word representations. It is important that the psychological set generally activated by a particular word be "correct" (that is, represent the intended entity). Of course, the psychological set activated by a particular word differs for different people.

Creating a word with the correct psychological set can be difficult. Often it is easy to pick a word with a "close" but dangerously "incorrect" psychological set. As an example, suppose a programmer decided to represent a deck of sale transaction cards, one of their unit records, and the unit record's three fields (the identification of a salesperson, the identification of the item sold, and the quantity of the item sold) with the respective words INPUT-CARD-FILE, INPUT-CARD-REC, FIELD-1, FIELD-2, and FIELD-3. The words INPUT-CARD-FILE and INPUT-CARD-REC might cause a reader to associate an arbitrary deck of cards with input data. A better choice would be words like SALE-TRANSACTION-FILE and SALE-TRANSACTION-REC. Likewise, the data names FIELD-1, FIELD-2, and FIELD-3, are not as informative as SALES-PERSON-ID-NUM, ITEM-ID-NUM, and QTY-SOLD.

Words like FIELD-1, FIELD-2, and FIELD-3 should be avoided for still another reason. For example, suppose that the format of a transaction card was changed so that the sales person identification number became the third field instead of the first field, and the item sold number became the first instead of the second field, etc. The word FIELD-1 must then be changed to FIELD-3, FIELD-2 to FIELD-1, etc. Needless to say, it is highly possible that some occurrence of the word FIELD-3 might not be changed to FIELD-1! Finding a mistake like the printer just made in the last sentence is another problem with such words.

Other examples of ill-considered words are the following:

SWITCH	What does SWITCH switch?
RMS-10	Too cryptic
NEXT-ADD	Is it next "addition" or next "address"?
GET-PROCESS-CARD	Should it be GET-AND-PROCESS-CARD or GET-PROCESSED-CARD?
REPORT-PROCESS	Are these nouns or verbs?

An important aspect of psychological set is the effect of abbreviations. Abbreviations are desirable in forming mnemonic user-defined words since COBOL tends to give rise to verbose programs. The first point to remember is that you should only abbreviate after you have created good mnemonic words. Second, choose only standard abbreviations; a dictionary is a good place to start. Third, the particular abbreviation chosen should not activate a psychological set different from the original word. Let us assume you have created the mnemonic (if lengthy) word OWNER-IDENTIFICATION-NUMBER and that it activates the correct psychological set. Assuming that you would like to shorten the word by abbreviating, you should reject such abbreviations as O-NO or OWN-ID-NUM, for they may very well be misleading. A word like OWNER-ID-NUM is preferable.

Psychological Distance

In addition to finding a proper word for each entity, you should choose words for different entities that are "psychologically distant" enough to avoid confusion. Since the distance concept is related to the psychology of the programmer, it resists formalization. Loosely speaking, words that look alike, sound alike, are spelled alike, or have similar meanings are not psychologically distant.

The abbreviation of words often causes problems with psychological distance. Consider the following pairs of words with an indication of their psychological distance:

Word for one entity	*Word for a different entity*	*Distance*
(a) WS-TFEES	WS-TFEESS	Almost zero
(b) LNC-TOTAL	LCN-TOTAL	Very little
(c) PROFITS-P1	PROFITS-P2	Little
(d) FACTOR	GROSS	Large
(e) OVERTIME-FACTOR	GROSS-PAY	Large and informative

Entries (a) and (b) show two different words which look and sound alike. Because these words are difficult to distinguish, so are the entities they represent. Only in entries (d) and (e) is the psychological distance significant.

Other Considerations

A programmer should also insure that all user-defined words exhibit "uniformity." This is also a difficult notion to formalize. In rough terms, all user-defined words that imply similar properties should be of similar form. For example, consider the previous sales transaction example. It would be unfortunate to choose the words,

SALESPERSON-ID-NUMBER
ITEM-NUM.

even though they can activate the correct psychological set and are psychologically distant, for this pair of data names does not follow a uniform coding scheme. A better choice of words is

SALESPERSON-ID-NUM
ITEM-ID-NUM.

The programmer is especially advised to keep abbreviations uniform.

Before using a word in a COBOL program, the programmer should also make sure that it is not a system name or a COBOL reserved word. It is handy to keep a list of reserved-words like those given in Fig. 5.1 and a list of system names.

The COBOL qualification capability is an excellent aid in choosing a user-defined word to represent an entity. If two items in two different records are the same, then a programmer can represent them with the same mnemonic word. There is no need to add a few extra code characters to these words to make them unique. The use of an "OF" or "IN" phrase will activate the correct psychological set easily. For example, consider the merits of

COMPUTE NIR-QTY-IN-STOCK = OIR-QTY-IN-STOCK − QTY-SOLD.

versus

COMPUTE QTY-IN-STOCK IN NEW-INVENTORY-REC =
QTY-IN-STOCK IN OLD-INVENTORY-REC − QTY-SOLD.

In conclusion, we probably cannot overemphasize the desirability of using good mnemonic user-defined words. In conjunction with good prettyprinting, they allow a programmer to take a huge step toward producing high quality, self-documenting code.

THE OVERCONCERN WITH MICRO-EFFICIENCY

Machine efficiency has been one of the most frequent concerns of managers and programmers alike. In the early years of computing, when hardware configurations were small and ran slow, it was important to use as little storage space or computer time as possible. Since then, digital computers have become large, inexpensive, and fast. In addition, virtual memory has been incorporated into many systems. Yet managers and COBOL programmers are still often concerned with the question of machine efficiency because of the need to control programming costs.

The reasons for striving after machine efficiency are not only historic and economic, for there is also a certain human element. Programmers take pride in their ability to squeeze out excess lines of code or to use an appropriate efficiency feature, and managers take a natural pride in the speed of their programs or their compact use of storage.

ACCEPT	DATE-COMPILED	GENERATE
ACCESS	DATE-WRITTEN	GIVING
ADD	DAY	GO
ADVANCING	DE	GREATER
AFTER	DEBUG-CONTENTS	GROUP
ALL	DEBUG-ITEM	
ALPHABETIC	DEBUG-LINE	HEADING
ALSO	DEBUG-NAME	HIGH-VALUE
ALTER	DEBUG-SUB-1	HIGH-VALUES
ALTERNATE	DEBUG-SUB-2	
AND	DEBUG-SUB-3	I-O
ARE	DEBUGGING	I-O-CONTROL
AREA	DECIMAL-POINT	IDENTIFICATION
AREAS	DECLARATIVES	IF
ASCENDING	DELETE	IN
ASSIGN	DELIMITED	INDEX
AT	DELIMITER	INDEXED
AUTHOR	DEPENDING	INDICATE
	DESCENDING	INITIAL
BEFORE	DESTINATION	INITIATE
BLANK	DETAIL	INPUT
BLOCK	DISABLE	INPUT-OUTPUT
BOTTOM	DISPLAY	INSPECT
BY	DIVIDE	INSTALLATION
	DIVISION	INTO
CALL	DOWN	INVALID
CANCEL	DUPLICATES	IS
CD	DYNAMIC	
CF		JUST
CH	EGI	JUSTIFIED
CHARACTER	ELSE	
CHARACTERS	EMI	KEY
CLOCK-UNITS	ENABLE	
CLOSE	END	LABEL
COBOL	END-OF-PAGE	LAST
CODE	ENTER	LEADING
CODE-SET	ENVIRONMENT	LEFT
COLLATING	EOP	LENGTH
COLUMN	EQUAL	LESS
COMMA	ERROR	LIMIT
COMMUNICATION	ESI	LIMITS
COMP	EVERY	LINAGE
COMPUTATIONAL	EXCEPTION	LINAGE-COUNTER
COMPUTE	EXIT	LINE
CONFIGURATION	EXTEND	LINE-COUNTER
CONTAINS		LINES
CONTROL	FD	LINKAGE
CONTROLS	FILE	LOCK
COPY	FILE-CONTROL	LOW-VALUE
CORR	FILLER	LOW-VALUES
CORRESPONDING	FINAL	
COUNT	FIRST	MEMORY
CURRENCY	FOOTING	MERGE
	FOR	MESSAGE
DATA	FROM	MODE
DATE		MODULES

Fig. 5.1   *A list of reserved words in COBOL*

MOVE	RECORDS	STATUS
MULTIPLE	REDEFINES	STOP
MULTIPLY	REEL	STRING
	REFERENCES	SUB-QUEUE-1
NATIVE	RELATIVE	SUB-QUEUE-2
NEGATIVE	RELEASE	SUB-QUEUE-3
NEXT	REMAINDER	SUBTRACT
NO	REMOVAL	SUM
NOT	RENAMES	SUPPRESS
NUMBER	REPLACING	SYMBOLIC
NUMERIC	REPORT	SYNC
	REPORTING	SYNCHRONIZED
OBJECT-COMPUTER	REPORTS	
OCCURS	RERUN	TABLE
OF	RESERVE	TALLYING
OFF	RESET	TAPE
OMITTED	RETURN	TERMINAL
ON	REVERSED	TERMINATE
OPEN	REWIND	TEXT
OPTIONAL	REWRITE	THAN
OR	RF	THROUGH
ORGANIZATION	RH	THRU
OUTPUT	RIGHT	TIME
OVERFLOW	ROUNDED	TIMES
	RUN	TO
PAGE		TOP
PAGE-COUNTER	SAME	TRAILING
PERFORM	SD	TYPE
PF	SEARCH	
PH	SECTION	UNIT
PIC	SECURITY	UNSTRING
PICTURE	SEGMENT	UNTIL
PLUS	SEGMENT-LIMIT	UP
POINTER	SELECT	UPON
POSITION	SEND	USAGE
POSITIVE	SENTENCE	USE
PRINTING	SEPARATE	USING
PROCEDURE	SEQUENCE	
PROCEDURES	SEQUENTIAL	VALUE
PROCEED	SET	VALUES
PROGRAM	SIGN	VARYING
PROGRAM-ID	SIZE	
	SORT	WHEN
QUEUE	SORT-MERGE	WITH
QUOTE	SOURCE	WORDS
QUOTES	SOURCE-COMPUTER	WORKING-STORAGE
	SPACE	WRITE
RANDOM	SPACES	
RD	SPECIAL-NAMES	ZERO
READ	STANDARD	ZEROES
RECEIVE	STANDARD-1	ZEROS
RECORD	START	

Fig 5.1 A list of reserved words in COBOL (cont'd)

The Real Costs

While we do not at all question the need to reduce programming costs, we do believe that this concern is often focused on the wrong issues. For example, some typical concerns in COBOL programming are the following:

1. Subscripts or high computation items should be described using COMP SYNC.
2. Decimal points in related numeric items should be aligned.
3. The use of MOVE CORRESPONDING, COMPUTE, CALL, or PER-FORM verbs should be restricted.
4. IF statements should be organized so that the most frequent conditions are checked first.

These rules are intended to save space and execution time, thus lowering costs. Because of the often rather small and local savings afforded by the above techniques, we shall call the efficiency they provide "micro-efficiency" [Ref. A1]. With the development of inexpensive fast storage and virtual memory systems, the preoccupation with the size and speed of machine code would seem to have been dealt a death blow. Not so! COBOL shops still practice old habits.

The concern with micro-efficiency has often obscured the really important programming costs. The first issue is to understand the problem completely and to ensure that the resulting specification satisfies the user. The second issue is to produce high quality system design, clear code, and clear documentation. The final issue, and only if necessary, is to produce a fast or compact program.

While micro-efficient programs do help to reduce overall costs, in the larger perspective they are usually only a small factor. The total cost of a system includes the costs of promotion, time needed to understand user requirements, the development of clear and acceptable specifications, program writing, documentation, and above all, maintenance. If a proposed programming system is not acceptable to the ultimate user, further development is wasted. If specifications are not adequate, system development is often misdirected and delayed. If there is a failure to recognize exceptional conditions and different solution strategies, or if there is a poor initial design, the success of any development effort is undermined. Moreover, program development costs include programmer training, thinking time, coding time, and the time and effort needed to integrate a subsystem into an overall system. Documentation costs include the time needed to prepare reports, figures, and summaries of existing code.

In the life of many systems, the largest cost factor is system maintenance. Maintenance of an ill-conceived, poorly developed, poorly coded, or poorly documented system is expensive and time consuming at best. More typically, system performance is seriously degraded. Easy maintenance of itself can yield greater savings than micro-efficient program performance. To control programming costs, we must look in the right places.

Program Performance

There are, of course, cases where the costs of program performance are significant. Perhaps a given program will be run every day, a given data file may be accessed every hour, or fast memory may be scarce. In these cases, attention should be devoted to the *top* levels of program design where "macro-efficient" techniques can be applied.

It does little good to scatter time and space micro-efficiencies all over the code if the buffering or blocking techniques are not optimal. At an even higher level, buffering and blocking techniques will be of little avail if the entire system frequently needs to be restarted because of the errors due to the improper input of data. In such cases, perhaps several sequentially executed programs with local and less severe restraints should be designed, rather than one large program. At the highest level, if the whole program is more easily handled without a digital computer, all the concern with computer performance costs is meaningless.

A rather meaningful issue stems from the following observation. It is estimated that 90 percent of the CPU time in a program is spent within 10 percent of the code. If a programmer is faced with program performance demands, the first consideration should be *where* the program is spending its time. Micro-efficiency can then be spent on this 10 percent of the code.

Finally, if a program is designing low-level portions of code and really needs micro-efficient techniques, caution is still in order. Considerations such as page size matching or COMP-3 items can make a program quite machine dependent. Tight, tricky, micro-efficient code can be almost impossible for another person to understand. These performance savings may in the end raise the cost of program maintenance.

The overriding points of our discussion can be summarized as follows. The concern with program micro-efficiency is often short-sighted. The primary concern should be to consider overall system costs and to place major economic emphasis on earlier phases of program development. There is a lot of money being wasted in the production of poor definitions, poor designs, poor documentation, and in slipshod program development.

THE CASE AGAINST PROGRAM FLOWCHARTS

In 1947, H. H. Goldstine and J. von Neumann [Ref. G1] introduced a pictorial notation called a "flow diagram." Its purpose was to facilitate the translation of algorithms into machine language programs. The flow diagrams pictured the course of machine control through a sequence of steps and indicated the contents and change of items in storage. Since then these ideas and notations, along with various diagrams and charts used in business system analysis [Ref. C3], have been absorbed into almost all areas of electronic data

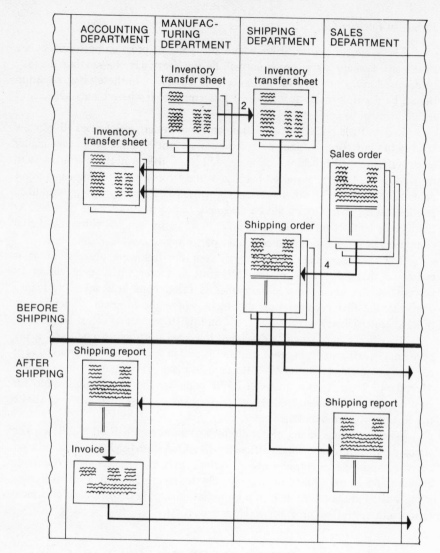

Fig. 5.2   A document flowchart

processing. The basic concept has come to be known as "flowcharting." We can roughly distinguish three types of flowcharts: document flowcharts, system flowcharts, and program flowcharts.

"Document" flowcharts primarily picture the movement of various documents (vouchers, invoices, purchase orders, reports, etc.) from department to department (group to group, or person to person) in an organization. An example is outlined in Fig. 5.2. Document flowcharts concentrate on the flow of data. Control flow (the time relation between actions) is not fully specified.

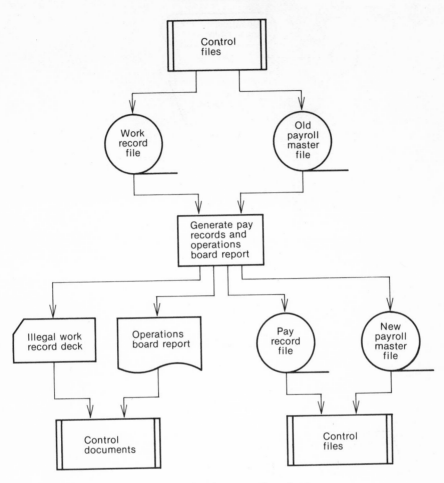

Fig. 5.3   A system flowchart

System flowcharts describe the flow of major data items and the control sequence of major operations in an information processing system. It is customary to picture the relationship existing between information, media, equipment, equipment operations, and manual operations. An example is given in Fig. 5.3. There are few specific details, and only a rough picture of the overall process. As with document flowcharts, system flowcharts concentrate more on the flow of data than on the flow of control.

Program flowcharts specify details of the sequential flow of control through an actual program. A familiar example is Fig. 5.4. Program flowcharts are the most direct descendant of Goldstine and von Neumann's flow diagrams, for both describe the flow of control in great detail. It is interesting to note that program flowcharts do not explicitly describe the data flow, as was the case with the original flow diagrams.

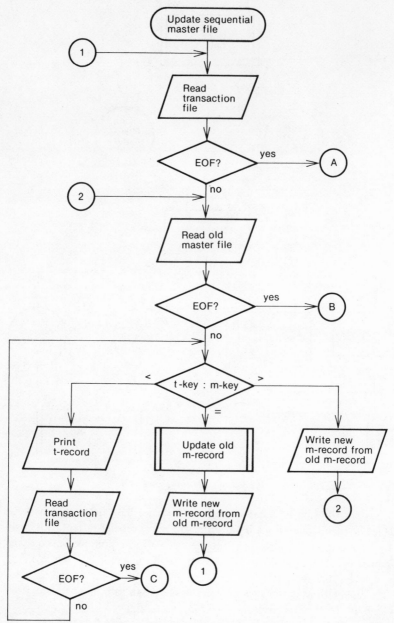

Fig. 5.4   A program flowchart

As for document and system flowcharts, we believe that they can be useful aids in describing systems and processes. For documentation, both types of flowcharts can give a quick synopsis of a process. Unfortunately, the use of these flowcharts has sometimes been mistaken for complete problem description.

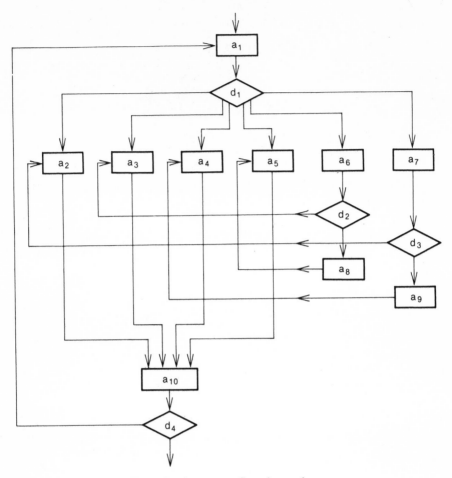

Fig. 5.5   A program flowchart schema

Our concern here is with program flowcharts, a technique familiar to all programmers and one often used daily. It is perhaps true that program flowcharts can assist in the design of very efficient, small algorithms. However, we believe that program flowcharts can easily suppress much useful information in favor of highlighting sequential control flow, something which distracts the programmer from the important functional relationship in the overall design. This in turn may obscure the use of alternative designs via the use of procedures and subprograms, the use of more intuitive data structures, or even the simple fine tuning of logic.

Consider the program flowchart schema in Fig. 5.5. The a_i stand for certain actions (for example, data moves or procedure calls); the d_i stand for decisions. The programmer who derived this flowchart was so concerned with lines and boxes (that is, sequences of steps) that the resulting code, while correct, tended to obscure the overall functional logic.

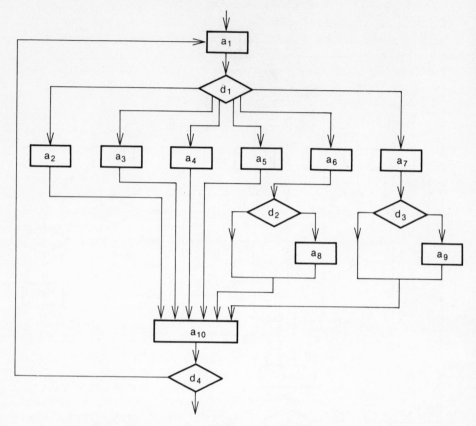

Fig. 5.6   Program flowchart schema derived from alternative code

Other design methods resulted in a different solution, which was not as brief as that obtained from program flowcharts, but easier to understand. Figure 5.6 is the picture of control flow derived from this new code.

One important problem with program flowcharts is keeping track of variables that change from one part of the flowchart to the next. A user who is preoccupied with flow of control details may quickly be in the position of the tourist to Boston who decides to drive his own car to see the sights. By not taking a sight-seeing bus, the visitor quickly gets distracted in the confusion of alternative routes.

Thinking back, were you ever asked to update or correct a program in which the documentation included program flowcharts? How often did you utilize them? Our observations indicate little such use of the charts. In the majority of cases the use of program flowcharts is replaced by a careful study of the code that produced them in the first place. Good code alone seems to be sufficient for the detailed understanding needed for program maintenance.

Program flowcharts have less severe deficiencies. One is a general untidiness caused by the simple human limitation in the art of drawing straight lines and figures, which makes flowcharting a time-consuming activity as well. Also, who in tarnation borrowed my template?

Besides its somewhat awkward notation, did you ever notice that a program flowchart always seems to spill over the margin of the paper used to draw it on? Look back at Figure 5.4. This flowchart requires numerous connectors and page skipping to read the result. After reading a few pages, who knows where you came from, never mind where you are going. Even if you manage to keep connectors to a minimum to prevent mental page flipping, data processing still involves many conditional checks (that is, branches) in flowcharts. When you connect all these branches to their logical destinations, you may find what is known as the "spaghetti effect," which is a profusion of crisscrossing branches (see Fig. 5.7).

Because of the rather large amount of time and work required to construct program flowcharts, program designers are naturally reluctant to rethink things and perhaps make a change or two. Even if a design modification is conceptually simple, the modification may require a flowchart box and line insertion that will force a complete redrawing just to get the chart to fit nicely on one page. When used for program documentation, what happens to flowcharts after a program modification? Even if someone else is assigned to update the program flowcharts, he or she may try to save time by squeezing in the modifications on the existing charts, perhaps in a different color ink. After a few years and many modifications one may have an interesting, modernistic work of art, but a very poor flowchart. If a flowchart generator program is available, this effect can admittedly be avoided; however, the results of flowchart generators are usually no more helpful than the original code.

In summary, programmers and managers should really think twice before using time and resources for constructing program flowcharts, whether it be for program design or documentation. For good program design we recommend the top-down approach, which is discussed in Chapter 3.

LARGE SYSTEMS

This book has focused on a single topic: the writing of quality programs by the individual programmer. The development of large software systems obviously involves other issues far beyond the scope of this book. But because of the importance of large systems, we introduce some of the quality issues here. Our ideas are based mainly on the papers by Cave [Ref. C1] and Cave and Ledgard [Ref. C2].

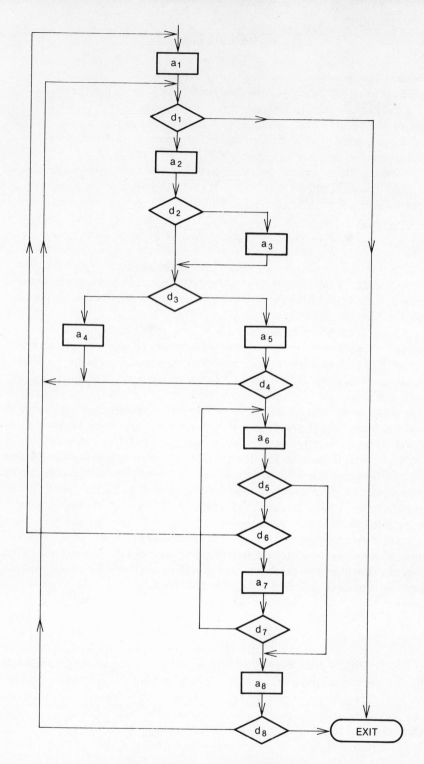

Fig. 5.7   Mild spaghetti effect

Premises

We begin with a number of premises that we believe are vital for the success of any large programming project.

1. The development of user-oriented software systems is first and foremost a management problem.

This is a difficult premise to accept because poor management reflects right to the top of any organization. Nevertheless, this premise is vital since project failures are generally the result of improper or inexperienced management and not a lack of technical ability. The management responsibility requires not only knowledge, experience, and judgment, but also a high level of perspective. To avoid major mistakes in policy, it is vital to have a good perspective of

a. The experience, skills, and tools required to complete a given task.
b. The availability of these resources within the organization.
c. The importance of establishing the credibility of outside experts through reliable references.
d. The need for constant vigilance against the dangers of sacrificing effectiveness for program efficiency.

2. The success of any software system is finally measured by the ultimate user.

In order for capable managers to succeed, they must have an environment that responds quickly and is controlled easily. The willingness on the part of prospective users to order and pay for services rendered on a continuing basis is the essential element for effective control. When "dollar control" flows directly from the end user down through the ranks of the developer, it creates an environment less prone to politics, cleverness, and internal disagreements.

Measuring management ability largely by user satisfaction also creates a willingness on the part of management to call on outside expertise and forces attention on the need for accurate performance measurement.

This environment concept closely relates to Baker's work [Refs. B1, B4]. The chief programmer team is organized around a chief with exceptional experience and control. One gets the feeling that this chief has one finger on the pulse of the entire project, while the tips of the other fingers control all members of the team. Within certain organizations, only a strong technical ability backed by strong personal credibility can create the environment needed to provide control and to obtain response from a team of programmers. The chief programmer team approach thus appears suitable for creating the management control essential to success in most organizations.

3. The overall project management must not be divorced from software development.

Independent of the individual system charactersitics, and a highly technical environment notwithstanding, overall project management must be directly responsible for developing the software.

First, it is all too easy to blame software failures on any organizational unit other than the one under question. Identifying the project management with the technical problems insures that management is indeed responsible for the entire effort.

Second, over and above the development of programs, the very nature of software development implies the need to develop the organization and managing procedures to be used in final operational systems. This decision-making process is implicitly given to the software developer. The reason, which is not readily apparent, is that the very nature of software development implicitly places the responsibility for designing a usable system upon those doing the creating, and not upon the user.

4. Software development must be a sequence of clearly isolated phases.

Changes *will* occur in project emphasis, personnel, time frames, user requirements, and the development environment. This implies that it is necessary to:

a. Allow time for the developer to gain experience and to discover the peculiarities of a given application.
b. Allow time to expose the user's personnel to relevant computer techniques.
c. Allow for well-controlled changes in user requirements
d. Allow for periodic reviews and GO-NOGO decisions after each design phase.

Only by a breakdown of the development effort into well-defined and clearly separate units can the problems of change be met.

5. An integrated set of standards must form the foundation for controlling the entire software development effort.

To acquire and maintain control, management must have the tools to impose a strict discipline at the very beginning. Strict standards are the key to this discipline. Typical standards include:

a. *Project Definition.* These standards specify the form for stating the objectives, constraints, and overall project plan.
b. *System Specification.* These standards focus on complete specifications of system characteristics.
c. *Documentation.* These standards must focus on complete specifications of system characteristics. The standards should insure that all documents are self-contained and read easily.
d. *Programming.* Generally these standards cover style, structure, and internal documentation of programs. Strict rules on the use of procedures, spacing and indentation, control structures, and choice of variable names are especially important. The ideal place to enforce these

standards is the language compiler. Barring that, program reading by managers and programmers is a good alternative.

e. *Testing and Quality Control.* Prior to coding, standard procedures must be established on developing test data and the buildup to a full cycle test. Good procedures for system modification and maintenance of the external documentation set must also be established prior to coding.

The Incremental Approach

We next outline an approach to the building of large systems that is based on the above premises. This approach, called the "Incremental Method," is due to Cave [Refs. C1 and C2]. It is incremental in the following senses:

a. It dictates a multiphase (not a single-phase) design effort.
b. Resources are committed on an incremental basis.
c. There are a series of clearly delineated review points.

Each phase follows a highly structured pattern of plan, do, write, and review.

Phase 1: Development of Project Objectives

The first phase is an explicit study of user objectives by the project management. Frequent contacts must be made with the user to develop a clear understanding of user problems. Emphasis must be placed on extracting relevant problem concerns and the elimination of arbitrary constraints that can only hamper further development. Hardware and software constraints must also be resolved. The result of this phase is a written description of user objectives. At this phase it may not be possible to estimate the entire system development costs. At the very least, a careful estimate must be made to determine the cost of the next phase.

Finally, both the user and developer must allow ample time to review the proposed objectives. If further development effort is justified, then the next phase can be executed.

Phase 2: Functional Specification

This phase focuses on a detailed analysis of user requirements. The result of this phase is a set of documents that functionally defines the entire system as seen by the user. We believe that this definition should be so complete that the specifications will ultimately serve as a basis for the user documentation.

In sharp contrast with many conventional system development procedures, this phase is precisely the time to prepare user manuals. It is unwise to proceed further without giving the ultimate user a detailed idea of what to expect from the proposed system. It is certainly easier to change an unsatisfactory design during this phase, rather than after coding.

Finally, a complete review must be undertaken to decide if the detailed specification is still acceptable to the user and still feasible from the viewpoint of the system designer.

Phase 3: Environment Specification

This phase is a period for determining environment requirements, such as equipment configurations, languages, and support software.

The first consideration should be a review of the existing technology. Trade-offs to meet the functional specification must be resolved. Any severe constraints on the hardware, support software, or operating system must be recognized. If the existing operating system or hardware requires major changes, then the cost of necessary changes must be defined.

The second concern should be the resolution of critical problems for which research or development is needed. Typical of such problems would be the development of unusual operating system algorithms or the design of a critical data structure for information storage and retrieval. Failure to resolve these problems early may undermine the success of the entire proposed system independently of the overall design approach.

Finally, a careful review should be undertaken to assess all required technical support. Any detected deficiencies in the hardware, operating system, or software support must be accounted for. Costs in time, people, and money should be estimated. Again, a GO-NOGO decision must be made by user and designer in concert.

Phase 4: System Design

This phase is devoted to detailed program documentation of the entire system and a matching of the design with effective personnel. The required programming personnel must first be given responsibility for documenting (before coding!) any proposed code. The procedures for doing this lie in the hands of the technical management. Each required document must be acceptable to management with full regard to the detailed functional specification standards.

It is important to stress the integration of individual involvement with the overall system documentation. Strict quality control must be placed on the system documentation from here on. Poor individual documentation will be a likely predictor of poor code, and any such low quality performance must be detected early. Any functional changes resulting from this phase must be incorporated in the design specifications themselves.

Finally, and again, is the review. A review at this point is critical, for significant software costs will be involved if progress to the next phase is agreed upon.

Phase 5: System Construction

This phase is primarily concerned with writing and testing the programs for the system. Because of the rather elaborate preparation of the previous phases, this phase should proceed must more smoothly and accurately than is generally expected. The first major concern is the adoption of strict programming standards. The standards should include the choice of a high-level language, programming techniques, restrictions on program spacing and indentation, control structures, and the organization of programming teams.

The second major concern is a strict scheduling of program assignments and the required hardware facilities. It is all too easy to accumulate day-by-day slippage due to improper coordination of program writing and hardware test facilities.

Formal modification procedures must be developed to process corrections, refinements, or user requests for changes. Continuous maintenance and "shakedown" of all the programming documentation is vital to the integrity of the whole design effort. Loss of control over this activity can only lead to a slow but steady erosion of product quality.

Finally, management and the user must make a GO-NOGO decision to field the system. If agreement is reached, the next phase is to proceed.

Phase 6: Real Environment Testing

During this period, the entire system is subjected to full-scale use under a simulated real user environment. The objective is the development of a full-cycle test whose effectiveness is satisfactory to both user and developer.

Representative user personnel are trained to use the system and shakedown the user's documentation. Formal modification procedures must be developed to process requests for corrections, refinements, and enhancements.

As the testing nears completion, detailed plans for the next phase, live operation, must be prepared. It is all too easy to let this planning fall by the wayside, but ultimately the user will have to live with the system. Planning should at least include cost estimates for steady state operation, and recovery procedures in case of system failure.

Finally, the user and developer must make the final GO-NOGO decision on whether to put the system into live operation or return to make changes.

Phase 7: Live Operation

If the preceding phases have been properly completed, live operation will be easily effected.

Formal procedures to determine responsibility for possible system errors and the corresponding correction process must be developed. The system maintenance agent as well as the user should be able to initiate correction requests. Formal procedures for processing requests for system refinements and enhancements must also be developed. If there are multiple systems in the field, these procedures must preserve the system identify and the integrity of the documentation. To reduce total documentation and program modification efforts, it may be desirable to accumulate modification requests as long as the system remains operable.

Last, the user and developer should periodically review the entire effort. The level and formality of reviews will, of course, vary. In any event, formal user/designer reviews should take place annually at a minimum.

Conclusions

There are no simple techniques for developing large systems of high quality. What we do maintain, however, is that there are viable management guidelines for acquiring and maintaining project control. These guidelines can be backed up by a clean breakdown of projects into distinct phases and a set of strict standards.

One important point must be noted. The crucial parameter for measuring project success is user satisfaction. However, when overall user requirements cause estimates of time, people, or funding to exceed imposed constraints, it is necessary that a decision be made to either relax the requirements or halt the project! The decision to continue a project under uncertain estimates of required costs definitely places the responsibility for possible excess on management's shoulders. It is, therefore, essential that any method for management control must allow for periodic continuation decisions so that halts can ensure a minimum waste of resources.

One of the initial difficulties of the approach given here is the notion of "front-end loading," or the rather large involvement with the early noncoding stages of a project. This concept is initially hard to accept. Especially under an incremental funding arrangement, it appears that the user is paying a high price in the beginning and getting little return. However, when the detailed documentation is completed (the end of the functional specification phase), users are generally enthusiastic about the approach.

PARTING COMMENTS

We close this chapter with a variety of thoughts alluded to in previous chapters. They are neither new nor rigorously supported, but they do sum up a number of important issues.

A controversial issue treated in this work is that of avoiding GO TO statements, which are widely used even by good programmers. The case against the GO TO is primarily based on its concentration on the flow of control rather than on the basic procedures needed to solve a given problem. If the programmer's real concern is to prevent a program from becoming opaque, then the indiscriminate use of the GO TO must stop. Except when required for illustrating the effects of the GO TO, we have not used GO TO's in this book. We recommend the same policy to the reader. We also believe that future versions of COBOL should provide a few more alternatives to the GO TO.

As mentioned in this chapter, the use of program flowcharts has been avoided in this text. As a method of program design, program flowcharts have been highly overvalued. The top-down approach to programming suppresses the use of these flowcharts in favor of highlighting a functional or procedural approach to program design. The case against program flowcharts is similar to the case against the GO TO. The lines and arrows can easily lead the user into a highly sequential mode of thinking. Furthermore, there is a tendency to think that once a program flowchart has been designed, the programming process is just about complete. Unfortunately, this is seldom the case. The programmer would be well-advised to try another approach whenever he thinks a program flowchart is needed.

An important and often undetected problem in writing good modular programs is the issue of data connections between modules. Suppose that a module M inputs a variable X and outputs a variable Y, with transfer of control always entering M at one point and always exiting M at one point. Simply satisfying this 1-in, 1-out transfer of control property does not guarantee that the module can be understood only in terms of the values of X and Y. If the code in M either depends on or alters variables outside of M, then the module is not isolated from changes in other modules. This difficulty frequently occurs in modules that refer to or alter global variables (variables common to everal modules) or modules that input new values from an external device. A problem arises when there are changes to the global variables or to the input data, for these changes may cause subtle effects on the functional relationship between X and Y. The simple rule of thumb is: Avoid designing modules with numerous data interconnections.

Consider the payroll program of Chapter 3. Each procedure fits on a page or less. This characteristic was deliberate. We all know how difficult it can be to write or read a long program. In any lengthy program, we usually try to abstract a logical portion of it that will give us an indication of its overall computation. Programmers should recognize this fact and write a program so that each logical unit is clearly isolated on a page or less. Furthermore, as mentioned above, each unit should be definable in terms of the fewest possible items it needs to use or change, for the excessive use of global variables can easily destroy the modularity of the logical units.

An interesting question is why COBOL is so popular even though the language has been around since 1960. The most obvious reason is that it was introduced with logical file, record, and item structures that were modeled for business applications. Other reasons are its adoption by the United States Government and the machine independence of its programs due to continuing standardization efforts. Also, the language has undergone steady modification and documentation by various committees in CODASYL and ANSI, with feedback coming from the user community as a whole. COBOL has thus achieved a reasonable and controlled rate of change. In short, COBOL still meets most business data processing needs.

The PL/I language was introduced with the hope that it would soon become familiar to most programmers and programming managers and eventually replace COBOL. This has not occurred, perhaps because PL/I is so complex that it is difficult to learn and to implement at a low cost, or perhaps because COBOL is an old friend, and you don't give up old friends easily.

However, COBOL lacks many now well-accepted features of other contemporary languages, among them being a case statement, internal procedures with explicit arguments, value returning procedures, and a provision for user-defined data types. The wordiness of COBOL, originally designed for the inexperienced and uninformed user, has become a problem as the language has grown. Coding, for the professional, is often tedious. There is a clear need for some major changes in COBOL to bring it in line with the many new ideas in contemporary programming.

The organization of numerous programmers into an effective programming team is a subject that also deserves much investigation. Large systems requiring thousands of lines of code are common. The notion that the requirements of a large programming project can be met simply by rapid staffing with large numbers of programmers is obsolete. Large amounts of verification time and poor code result from a lack of careful analysis of design and staffing. The concept of a "chief programmer team" advocated by Mills and Baker [Ref. B1] has had some strong initial success. Considering the importance of large systems, it is clearly worth the investment to try to develop standardized approaches to large programming projects.

There are many other issues that need to be investigated. Among these are the need for better documentation of programs, better programming languages, the establishment of problem definition techniques, the development of a more manageable successor to COBOL, and the promotion of human factors [Ref. L5]. The final issue is the critical need to upgrade the entire programming effort.

With all of the new interest in programming, progress is certainly on its way. We must discipline ourselves to this interest but only adopt what is really progress. Perhaps the best motivation is to recall how much hard work went into the last program you wrote and also that the program you write today may be the program you will maintain next year.

EXERCISES

Exercise 5.1

A programmer must guard against using words with incorrect psychological sets. The following code fragment is the Procedure Division of a subprogram called CALC-Y-INT. The inputs to the subprogram are two tables, P1 and P2, each of which consists of two entries. The outputs are the numbers INT, RATE, and the subprogram result flag RESULT-CODE-NUM. The familiar function of CALC-Y-INT is obscured by misleading and vague words. Rename the subprogram and rewrite the fragment using a better choice of mnemonic words.

```
MAIN-PROGRAM.
    IF   (P1(1) = P2(1))
        MOVE ZERO TO   INT, RATE
        MOVE 1 TO   RESULT-CODE-NUM
    ELSE
        COMPUTE NUM    = P1(2)  −  P2(2)
        COMPUTE DENOM = P1(1)  −  P2(1)
        COMPUTE RATE  = NUM / DENOM
        COMPUTE INT    = P1(2)  −  (RATE * P1(1) )
        MOVE ZERO TO   RESULT-CODE-NUM
    RETURN-TO-CALLER.
        EXIT PROGRAM.
```

Exercise 5.2

It is likely that you disagree strongly with at least one of the topics discussed in this chapter. Pick the one that you disagree with the most and prepare a comprehensive counterproposal. After the customary number of rewrites, have someone else read it. (Hint: Choose a friend to do the reading.) When you are finished, send the results to the authors of this book.

Exercise 5.3

This exercise is for those who have just completed reading our brief text. First, we want to thank you for the compliment of reading this book. Second, compare the style of the next COBOL program you write with one you wrote prior to reading our book. Evaluate the impact of our book on your COBOL programming style and send us a letter.

Exercise 5.4

Below are two advanced topics that we would have liked to discuss in this chapter. Pick the one that interests you the most, discuss the relevant issues, seek out the opinions of others, and present proposals which resolve some of the problems therein. Submit your results to a conference:

Topic 1: "The Problem with Problem Definition"

Issues: How should one detail inputs and outputs? What is a "functional" specification? What constitutes a "complete" definition? How much of a definition can be used for documentation? Where do implementation requirements go? What about condition-action lists versus decision tables? How should the layout and organization of a good, complete definition appear?

Topic 2: "The Global Variable Problem in COBOL"

Issues: Should COBOL allow arguments to procedures? Should the "scope" of variables be limited? Should programmers create unique names for each item or promote the use of the "qualified" names? Would any simple techniques or simple language changes prevent every variable from being global? Is "block structure" too extreme an aternative?

Exercise 5.5

Take the rest of the afternoon off. (We knew we could use this somewhere.)

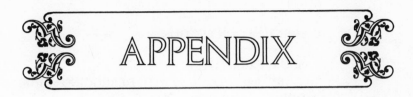

APPENDIX

PRETTYPRINTING STANDARD

General Rules

[GEN-1]   Between each division, section, or paragraph, there must be a page eject or a sequence of blank lines that is longer than the maximum sequence of blank lines within the previous division, section, or paragraph. The only exception is for empty or dummy paragraphs.

[GEN-2]   Use at least one blank line between a division header and the first non-blank line of the division.

[GEN-3]   Place division and section headers on a line by themselves starting at position 8.

[GEN-4]   Place paragraph headers and paragraph names on a line by themselves.

[GEN-5]   Do not break words or numeric literals across lines.

[GEN-6]   The text of every comment line must begin with "**" and must not be aligned with surrounding program text. For example, use

```
*      ** COMPUTE NET-PAY USING SCHEDULE 141-01-75.
    COMPUTE RELIEF-DEDUCT = GROSS-PAY * RELIEF-FUND-RATE.
```

           not

```
*    COMPUTE NET-PAY USING SCHEDULE 141-01-75.
    COMPUTE RELIEF-DEDUCT = GROSS-PAY * RELIEF-FUND-RATE.
```

[GEN-7]   Continuation lines must be indented at least two spaces from the starting position of the initial line.

Environment Division

[ENV-1]   Place main clauses (for example, SELECT clauses) and computer names on separate lines starting at position 12.

[ENV-2]   Place subclauses on separate lines indented at least two spaces from position 12. For example (see also ENV-1), use:

```
8     12
↓     ↓
CONFIGURATION SECTION.

    SOURCE-COMPUTER
    IBM-360   MODEL-50 WITH DEBUGGING MODE.
    OBJECT-COMPUTER.
    IBM-360   MODEL-50,
    MEMORY SIZE 32768 WORDS.

INPUT-OUTPUT SECTION.

    FILE-CONTROL.
    SELECT TRANSACTION-FILE
        ASSIGN TO SYS088-UR-254.
    SELECT OLD-INVENTORY-FILE
        ASSIGN TO SYS011-UT-166.
```

Data Division

[DATA-1]   Independent data division aggregates (i.e. FD, SD, CD, and RD entries along with their following data description entries) must be separated by a page eject or a sequence of blank lines longer than the maximum sequence of blank lines within the previous aggregate.

[DATA-2]   Consider placing at least one blank line before each level 01 data description entry.

[DATA-3]   Start level indicators (FD, SD, CD, RD) and 01 level numbers at position 10.

[DATA-4]   The level numbers of immediately subordinate items of a group item must be indented at least two spaces (possibly four) from the starting position of the level number of the group item. For example,

```
01   WORK-CARD.
     02   HOURS-WORKED  PICTURE 9(3)V9(2).
     02   FIRST-NAME    PICTURE X(20).
     02   LAST-NAME     PICTURE X(20).
```

[DATA-5]   In an FD, SD, CD, or RD entry with multiple clauses, place each clause on a separate line, indenting each clause at least two spaces from the starting position of the entry name. For example, use:

```
FD OLD-INVENTORY-FILE
   LABEL RECORDS ARE STANDARD,
   BLOCK CONTAINS 10 RECORDS,
   RECORD CONTAINS 95 CHARACTERS.
```

        not

```
FD OLD-INVENTORY-FILE   LABEL RECORDS ARE STANDARD, BLOCK
   CONTAINS 10 RECORDS, RECORD CONTAINS 95 CHARACTERS.
```

[DATA-6]   Wherever possible, nonnumeric literals of a VALUE clause must not be split onto a continuation line. For example,

pos 72
↓

```
01   SOC-SEC-NUM-LINE.
  02   FILLER        PICTURE  X(15), VALUE SPACES.
  02   CAPTION       PICTURE  X(25), VALUE "SOCIAL SECURITY NU
       "MBER  :  ".
  02   SOC-SEC-NUM   PICTURE  9(9).
```

is not allowed.

[DATA-7]   If the descriptive clauses of a data description entry do not fit on one line, an attempt should be made to indent the starting positions of continuation lines at least two spaces from the starting position of the initial descriptive clause. For example,

```
01   SOC-SEC-NUM-LINE.
  02   FILLER        PICTURE   X(15), VALUE SPACES.
  02   CAPTION       PICTURE   X(25),
                     VALUE "SOCIAL SECURITY NUMBER  :  ".
  02   SOC-SEC-NUM   PICTURE   9(9).
```

is preferred over

```
01   SOC-SEC-NUM-LINE.
  02   FILLER        PICTURE   X(15), VALUE SPACES.
  02   CAPTION       PICTURE   X(25),
       VALUE "SOCIAL SECURITY NUMBER  :  ".
  02   SOC-SEC-NUM   PICTURE   9(9).
```

Procedure Division

[PROC-1]   Begin each statement on a new line.

[PROC-2]   Align the starting positions of the statements making up a sentence and the sentences making up a paragraph. The general rule is to align logically parallel constructs.

[PROC-3]   The word "ELSE" in a conditional statement is to be aligned with the corresponding word "IF". The statements in the IF part and the ELSE part must be indented ast least two spaces. For example (see also PROC-2), use:

```
IF (WEIGHTED-SUM-ERROR)
    MOVE 1  TO  CHECK-DIGIT-CONDITION
ELSE
    MOVE 0  TO  CHECK-DIGIT-CONDITION
    DIVIDE  WEIGHTED-SUM  BY DESIRED-MODULUS
        GIVING  INTEGER-QUOTIENT
```

```
            REMAINDER   INTEGER-REMAINDER
     COMPUTE CALC-CHECK-DIGIT   =
            DESIRED-MODULUS   -   INTEGER-REMAINDER.
```

not

```
IF(WEIGHTED-SUM-ERROR)   MOVE 1 TO   CHECK-DIGIT-CONDITION
ELSE MOVE 0   TO   CHECK-DIGIT-CONDITION
     DIVIDE WEIGHTED-SUM BY   DESIRED-MODULUS GIVING
          INTEGER-QUOTIENT
     REMAINDER INTEGER-REMAINDER
     COMPUTE CALC-CHECK-DIGIT   =   DESIRED-MODULUS   -
          INTEGER-REMAINDER.
```

[PROC-4]   Place phrases such as AT END, WHEN, INVALID KEY, GIVING, USING, TALLYING, VARYING, UNTIL, and AFTER on separate lines, indenting the start of each phrase at least two spaces to the right. For example, use

```
PERFORM   TALLY-EMPLOYEE-DATA
     VARYING   TABLE-SUBSCRIPT   FROM 1 BY 1
     UNTIL   (TABLE-SUBSCRIPT > SIZE-EMPLOYEE-TABLE).
```

not

```
PERFORM TALLY-EMPLOYEE-DATA VARYING TABLE-SUBSCRIPT
FROM 1 BY 1 UNTIL (TABLE-SUBSCRIPT > SIZE-EMPLOYEE-TABLE).
```

[PROC-5]   Each procedure (level 2) performed by the main program (level 1) must be listed immediately after the main program. Subsequent procedures (level 3) performed by procedures in level 2 must be listed just after level 2, etc. Within levels, the order of listing is up to the user. For example:

```
*          **   MAIN PROGRAM, LEVEL 1
     A1.
          PERFORM B1.
          PERFORM B2.
          PERFORM B3.
          . . .
*            **   LEVEL 2 PROCEDURES

     B1.
          PERFORM D1.
          PERFORM C1.
          . . .
     B2.
          PERFORM D1.
          . . .
     B3.
          . . .
```

```
*           **  LEVEL 3 PROCEDURES
     C1.
           PERFORM D1.
           . . .
     C2.
           . . .
*           **  SPECIAL PROCEDURES
     D1.
           . . .
```

There are two allowed exceptions: (1) Procedures called from several levels and (2) procedures that are logically related (e.g., I-O routines). These may be grouped as desired by the programmer.

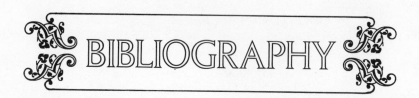

BIBLIOGRAPHY

[A1] Armstrong, Russel M., *Modular Programming In COBOL*, Business Data Processing, John Wiley & Sons, New York, 1973.

[B1] Baker, F. T., "Chief Programmer Team Management of Production Programming," *IBM Systems Journal*, vol. II, No. 1, 1972.

[B2] Berkowitz, M., *A Study and Design of COBOL Pre-compilers*, University of Massachusetts Master's Project, Department of Computer and Information Science, 1972.

[B3] Boehm, Barry W., "Software and Its Impact: A Quantitive Assessment *Datamation*, vol. 19, No. 5, May 1973.

[B4] Brooks, Fredrick P., Jr., *The Mythical Man-Month*, Addison-Wesley Publishing Co., Reading, Mass., 1975.

[C1] Cave, William C., "A Method for Management Control of Software System Development," CENTACS Software Report, No. 41, U.S. Army Electronics Div., Fort Monmouth, NJ, 1974.

[C2] Cave, William C., and Ledgard, Henry F., "Success is Not Beyond Our Control," Unpublished paper, University of Massachusetts, Amherst, 1974.

[C3] Cougar, J. Daniel, "Evolution of Business System Analysis Techniques," *Computing Surveys*, vol. 5, No. 3, Sept. 1973.

[D1] Dahl, O. J., Dykstra, E. W., and Hoare, C. A. R., *Structured Programming*, Academic Press, New York, 1972.

[G1] Goldstine, H. H., and von Neumann, J., "Planning and Coding for an Electronic Computing Instrument—Part II, Volume I," *John von Neumann—Collected Works*, Vol. V, Pergamon Press, New York, 1963.

[H1] Hicks, H. T., Jr., "Using the COBOL Report Writer," *Datamation*, vol. 18, No. 9, Sept. 1972.

[K1] Katzenelson, J., "Documentation and the Management of a Software Project—A Case Study," *Software—Practice and Experience*, vol. 1, 147–157, 1971.

[L1] Ledgard, Henry F., *Programming Proverbs*, Hayden Books, Rochelle Park, N.J., 1975.

[L2] Ledgard, Henry F., *Programming Proverbs for FORTRAN Programmers*, Hayden Books, Rochelle Park, N.J., 1975.

144

[L3] Ledgard, Henry F., and Marcotty, Michael, "A Genealogy of Control Structures," *Communications of the ACM*, Nov. 1975.

[L4] Ledgard, Henry F., and Cave, William C., "COBOL Calligraphy," Technical Report, Computer Software Team, U.S. Army Electronics Div., Fort Monmouth, N.J., 1975.

[L5] Ledgard, Henry F., Singer, A., and Hueras, J., "The Programmer's Assistant," COINS Technical Report, University of Massachusetts, 1976.

[L6] London, K. R., *Documentation Standards—Revised Edition*, Petrocelli Books, New York, 1974.

[M1] McCracken, D. D., and Garbassi, U., *A Guide to COBOL Programming*, 2nd ed., Wiley-Interscience, John Wiley & Sons, Inc., New York, 1970.

[M2] Mills, Harlan D., *Mathematical Foundations of Structured Programming*, Technical Report FSC 72-6012, IBM Federal Systems Div., Gaithersburg, Md. 1972.

[N1] Nattaly, S. M., Cohen, M. C., and Johnson, B. B., *COBOL Support Packages . . . Programming and Productivity Aids*, John Wiley & Sons, Inc., New York, 1972.

[S1] Spier, Michael J., *The Typset-10 Codex Programmaticus*, Technical Report, Digital Equipment Corp., 1974.

[S2] Stevenson, Henry, ed., *Structured Programming in COBOL*, Proceedings of a Symposium, Los Angeles, 1975. Available from ACM Order Dept., Box 12105, Church Street Station, New York, N.Y.

[T1] Thierauf, R. J., *Data Processing for Business and Management*, John Wiley & Sons, Inc., New York, 1973.

[W1] Weinberg, Gerald M., *The Psychology of Computer Programming*, Computer Science Series, Van Nostrand, Reinhold Co., New York, 1971.

[W2] Wigg, J. D., "COBOL Coding Standards," *The Computer Bulletin*, July, 1971.

[W3] Wirth, Nicklaus, "Program Development by Stepwise Refinement," *Communications of the ACM*, vol. 14, No. 4, April 1971.

[W4] Woolley, G. W., *Contemporary COBOL*, Rinehart Press, San Francisco, Cal., 1971.

[Y1] Yourdon, E., *Techniques of Program Structure and Design*, Prentice-Hall, Inc., N.J., 1975.

[Z1] _____, *American National Standard Programming Language COBOL*, *X.3.23-1974*, American National Standards Institute, Inc., 1430 Broadway, New York, N.Y. 10018.

[Z2] _____, "Modular COBOL Programming," *EDP Analyser*, July 1972.

[Z3] _____, *American National Standard Flowchart Symbols and Their Usage In Information Processing*, American National Standards Institute, Inc., 1430 Broadway, New York, N.Y. 10018.

[Z4] _____, "That Maintenance 'Iceberg'," *EDP Analyzer*, Oct. 1972.

INDEX